NATIONAL ECONOMIC DEVELOPMENT OFFICE

E FUTURE
TTERN OF
SHOPPING

Distributive Trades EDC

London, Her Majesty's Stationery Office 1971

National Economic Development Office
Millbank Tower, Millbank
London s w 1
01–834 3811
April 1971

Contents

CONTENTS—*continued*

Foreword

by Sir Bernard Miller,
Chairman,
Shopping Capacity Sub-Committee

This Report attempts to distil, partly from the statistical and other evidence already available and partly from fresh research into facts and opinions, some guidance upon the factors which should be taken into account in planning the nation's shops during the next decade. In this period there will be very great change and development in retail distribution, and it is correspondingly important that the decisions that determine it shall be properly based.

Many interests will be concerned in these decisions – multiple shops, independent retailers, consumers, property developers, economic development consultants, local authorities and central government. This report results from the work of a committee on which all of these interests have been represented: at various times nearly forty people have served either upon the committee or upon working groups set up by it.

Effective shop planning requires close teamwork between private enterprise and the public authorities, the former concerned with assessing the need for, and economics of, shopping development and the latter concerned with the relationship of shopping development to the total environment and to all the social needs of the community. For this teamwork to be properly effective there must be adequate data for valid assessment of both the public and the private interests.

One clear result of our work, although sadly a negative one, has been to highlight the inadequacy of the data upon which any effective shop planning must be based. This cannot be put right quickly and no time should be lost before taking the necessary steps to make it possible in the future.

There are in this country at present no institutions that provide the kind of framework for collaboration between private enterprise and public authorities in shop planning such as exists in the Danish Institute of Centre Planning or in the co-operation of public and private planning in Sweden. In this area the report urges the desirability and value of guidelines upon public policy being made available to private planners and the value that some research and planning institution, as a combined public authority/private enterprise project, could have.

It is the hope of the Shopping Capacity Sub-Committee that this report will stimulate the further action that alone can make the work of the committee really fruitful: its value will depend upon its effect in stimulating the work which remains to be done and which must be done if retailing is to be efficient and economic for the entrepreneur and shopping attractive and satisfying for consumers.

It remains for me to thank the members of the sub-committee and its working groups for the great amount of time and trouble that they gave to our work. In particular I wish to thank the members of the Models Working Group and its chairman, Professor Lichfield, for their work in the production of the report *Urban Models in Shopping Studies** published in September 1970. Our thanks are due also to the Research Institute for Consumer Affairs for making available to us the results of their shopping surveys in Norwich and Stevenage: this work provided a valuable insight into consumer attitudes. Thanks are also due to the many bodies given in our list of acknowledgements; these were not represented on the sub-committee but helped us greatly by providing information and carrying out work on our behalf: particular thanks are due to the local authorities who co-operated with us in the surveys of retailers.

Above all, I am glad to acknowledge here my own and the committee's debt to our Secretary, Mr Ian Helps, and to the staff of the NEDO office who have assisted him. He has been responsible for the drafting of the report and, with the staff, has serviced and sustained the committee throughout: an arduous and difficult task which has been admirably discharged.

Any committee report tends to be a compromise between the different ideas of its members. In this committee there was, of course, divergence of views and of emphasis but we reached in discussion a high degree of common agreement which must add weight to the report. I, as their Chairman, am deeply grateful to all of the members of the committee upon whose expertise, forbearance and unfailing helpfulness in carrying the work to a conclusion I have thankfully depended.

---

* *Urban Models in Shopping Studies,* available from NEDO price 70p

Membership of Shopping Capacity Sub-Committee and Working Groups

Shopping Capacity Sub-Committee (as at 31 July, 1970)

Chairman

Sir Bernard Miller — Chairman, John Lewis Partnership

Members

J H H Baxter	Ministry of Transport
H D G Collings	Department of Trade and Industry
M Grainger	Estate Manager, W H Smith & Son Ltd
Lady Hall	NEDO and Somerville College, Oxford
G R Hopkins	Former Director, Lewis's Ltd
Lord Jacques	Chairman, Co-operative Union
Dr J B Jefferys	Secretary-General, International Association of Department Stores
D H Lamb	Managing Director, Gateway (J H Mills) Ltd
Professor N Lichfield	University College, London, and Nathaniel Lichfield and Associates
F P W Maynard	Director, Ravenseft Properties Ltd
S W Perring	Managing Director, W Perring and Co Ltd (until September 1968)
J Phillips	Assistant General Secretary, Union of Shop, Distributive and Allied Workers
K R Read	NEDO
Miss Eirlys Roberts	Consumers' Association, Editor of 'Which?'
W K Shepherd	Estates & Development Valuer, City of Plymouth
E G Sibert	Surrey County Planning Officer
A Strachan	Department of the Environment
D C Stroud	Department of the Environment
P R V Watkins	Partner, Jno Oliver Watkins & Sons, Estate Agents
Professor C B Winsten	Nuffield College, Oxford, and University of Essex

Secretary

I G Helps — NEDO

Models Working Group (as at 31 December, 1969)

Chairman

Professor N Lichfield — University College, London, and Nathaniel Lichfield and Associates

Vice-Chairman

Professor C B Winsten — Nuffield College, Oxford, and University of Essex

Members

Professor S Eilon	Imperial College, London
Mr R Evely	Development Analysts Ltd
Mr T Gregory	City Planning Officer, Coventry
Lady Hall	NEDO and Somerville College, Oxford
Mr H Jones (up to June 1968)	Planning Department, GLC
Mr E Parkinson	City Planning Officer, Cardiff
Dr J R L Schneider	Board of Trade Census Office
Mr A L Strachan	Ministry of Housing and Local Government
Mr D C Stroud	Department of Economic Affairs
Miss J M Willson (from June 1968)	Planning Department, GLC
Mr A G Wilson	Centre for Environmental Studies

Secretary

Mr J R Donnison	NEDO

Future Pattern of Retailing Working Group

Chairman

Lady Hall	NEDO and Somerville College, Oxford

Members

Dr J B Jefferys	Secretary-General, International Association of Department Stores
Professor N Lichfield	University College, London, and Nathaniel Lichfield and Associates
Mr J de Somogyi	Marks and Spencer Ltd
Mr A Strachan	Ministry of Housing and Local Government

Secretary

Mr I G Helps	NEDO

Sales per Square Foot Working Group (as at 31 March, 1970)

Chairman

Professor C B Winsten	Nuffield College, Oxford, and University of Essex

Members

Dr D Diamond	London School of Economics
Mr A P McAnally	John Lewis Partnership
Mr W K Shepherd	Estates and Development Valuer, City of Plymouth
Mr A A Way	Essex Deputy County Planner

Secretary

Mr I G Helps	NEDO

Acknowledgements

Writing this report has involved contact with many individuals and organisations without whose co-operation its publication would have been impossible. We would like to thank a large number of retail firms and the following organisations not directly represented on the sub-committee for the time and trouble their representatives gave to helping us.

Central government bodies
The Road Research Laboratory
The Building Research Station

Local authorities and New Town corporations
Basildon Development Corporation
Chester City Council
Cumbernauld Development Corporation
Derby County Borough Council
Doncaster County Borough Council
Hertfordshire County Council
Jarrow Municipal Borough Council
Lancashire County Council
The Greater London Council
Norwich City Council
Portsmouth City Council
Preston County Borough Council
Runcorn Development Corporation
Stevenage Development Corporation
West Riding of Yorkshire County Council

Trade associations etc
Co-operative Union
Retail Alliance
Drapers' Chamber of Trade
Menswear Association of Great Britain
Multiple Shops Federation
National Association of Retail Furnishers
National Federation of Ironmongers
National Chamber of Trade
National Pharmaceutical Union
Radio and Television Retailers' Association
Retail Distributors' Association

Property developers
Arndale Property Trust Limited
Capital and Counties Property Company Limited
Grosvenor Estate Commercial Developments Limited
The Hammerson Group of Companies
Yorktown Developments Limited

Economic development consultants	Donaldson and Sons Development Analysts Limited Drivers, Jonas and Company Economic Consultants Limited Gerald Eva and Company Goddard and Smith Graves, Son and Pilcher National Cash Register Company Limited
University departments	Department of Applied Economics, Cambridge Distributive Trades Research Unit, Durham Department of Management Studies, Leeds Department of Economics, Leicester
Other bodies	Institut for Center Planlaegning, Denmark Institute of Food Distribution Lintas Special Projects Limited Town Planning Institute

Chapter 1 Introduction

The Shopping Capacity Sub-Committee was set up by the Economic Development Committee for the Distributive Trades in October 1966.

When the structure of the distributive trades was considered by the EDC – the structure of their several industries being a 'remit' to all EDCs – it was suggested that this structure could not be discussed fruitfully till the EDC had a clearer idea of what the pattern and capacity* of shopping was going to be in the future. Many retailers, government departments, property development companies, academics, and economic development consultants appeared to be thinking about the future shape and size of shopping capacity, but there seemed to be no existing organisation for bringing this thinking together so that it could be discussed.

There was also concern regarding the structure for the strategic planning of the nation's shopping requirements. In comprehensive development areas and in new towns the Secretary of State for the Environment exercises control over the amount and location of shopping floorspace. Elsewhere, however, although development plans require his approval, he is primarily concerned with broad land uses and planning strategy, and only when there is an appeal against a refusal by the local planning authority to grant planning permission, or when an application is 'called in' for consideration by the Department, does the Secretary of State exercise detailed control in the siting and quantity of shopping. The Department does of course operate in an advisory capacity.

The EDC was also concerned about the fears expressed in some quarters that there was a grave danger of too much shopping capacity being provided for the country as a whole, while still leaving some areas with inadequate shopping facilities.

The EDC therefore decided to set up a Shopping Capacity Sub-Committee with the following terms of reference:

To consider and advise the EDC on:

1 The work going on in government departments, universities and private firms which indicates the future pattern and capacity of shopping.

2 What the pattern and capacity of shopping is likely to be in 10 to 20 years time, assuming legislation is unchanged, based on the views of organisations, on extrapolation of past trends, and the relevant experience of other countries.

3 What pattern and capacity of shopping would provide the best use of resources, economic efficiency and the greatest convenience to customers.

---

* For this and other technical terms see Glossary on page 79

4   In what ways (2) and (3) can be brought closer together.
5   What implications the above have for current and future urban physical and economic planning policies.

The first of the sub-committee's terms of reference asked it to advise the EDC on the work going on in government departments, universities and private firms which indicates the future pattern and capacity of shopping.

This work can be considered under two headings:

(a)   Theoretical work directed at the construction of mathematical models seeking to interpret and predict the way shoppers, retailers and shopping centres impinge upon each other. This area was considered by the Models Working Group, and a report containing the results of their work was published as *Urban Models in Shopping Studies,* 1970

(b)   Other work directed at various aspects of the provision of shopping capacity. A list of research projects known to us in June 1970 will be found in Appendix A.

The points arising from the other terms of reference are examined in the remaining chapters of this report, a summary of the principal findings being contained in Chapter 2.

Chapter 3 deals with likely changes in the pattern of retailing in the UK: our conclusions here are largely based on a questionnaire sent to retailers, planning officers and other interested parties.

Chapter 4 examines floorspace requirements in the UK in 1980. It begins by presenting a forecast of what consumers' expenditure in real terms is likely to be in 1980, based on an analysis carried out for the sub-committee by the Department of Applied Economics at Cambridge. An examination of the intensity of use of floorspace follows: this includes a review of the data available, and an estimate of the rate of change of floorspace utilisation calculated as sales value achieved per square foot of selling space (ie 'sales per square foot'). The chapter concludes by relating the floorspace estimated to be required (on the basis of changes in consumers' expenditure, floorspace utilisation and population) to the floorspace which seems likely to exist given the continuation of existing nett rates of building, and discusses the consequences.

Chapter 5 examines the reasons for success or failure of shopping centres, and isolates what, on the basis of analytical work, appear to be the salient factors: these points must receive the closest attention if the best use is to be made of resources.

Chapter 6 considers the types of location where shopping will be carried out by 1980, and suggests where the greatest emphasis needs to be laid in development.

Chapter 7 examines the present planning mechanism in this country and the way it is operated.

Lastly, Chapter 8 indicates the need for co-ordination of further work in this field and considers what is the best way of achieving this.

Chapter 2 Findings and recommendations

Findings   The work undertaken by the Shopping Capacity Sub-Committee suggests that the following conclusions may be drawn about changes which may be anticipated by 1980:

1   We estimate that consumers' expenditure in shops* will increase from about £9,800 million in 1968 to between £13,000 million and £14,500 million (at 1963 prices): this represents an annual rate of increase of about 2.3 per cent and 3.3 per cent respectively. The proportion of this increased expenditure spent on food, drink and tobacco will diminish, while that spent on non-food goods will increase.

2   It would appear, from the rather limited information available to us, that floorspace utilisation is currently rising by about 1.0 per cent per annum in food shops and 1.5 per cent per annum in non-food shops. (This relates to gross floorspace† within the curtilage of the shop: it does not relate to warehouses etc in separate buildings.)

3   We calculated the floorspace that will be required in 1980 on the basis of anticipated trends in (a) consumers' expenditure in shops per head of population, (b) utilisation of floorspace and (c) population changes (see Appendix E). Comparison of these figures with the latest nett annual rate of increase of floorspace in England and Wales (1964–7) suggests that extrapolation of the latter trend at a constant rate would result in floorspace higher than that required. (This conclusion applied to all of England and Wales except East Anglia, where the Registrar-General forecasts much the largest increase in population in the whole country.) This conclusion should not be interpreted as suggesting that this country will be 'over-shopped' in 1980 in the sense that shops in town centres will be standing vacant; rather, it suggests either that the rate of new building will be cut back, or that the rate of obsolescence will accelerate and increasing numbers of shops in marginal locations (especially 'street-corner' shops in areas adjacent to town centres) will be demolished or converted to other uses. (We have not been able to carry out work on the question of what is the optimal rate of obsolescence or what margin of 'spare' capacity is necessary to cater for changing circumstances: these are, however, subjects which might be studied with useful results.)

4   There is already evidence that many shops in marginal locations ('street-corner' shops and areas adjacent to town centres) are finding it increasingly difficult to survive. This problem is likely to be considerably exacerbated if, as was suggested in the previous paragraph, there is an acceleration of the rate of obsolescence. This

---

* See Appendix D for definition
† See Glossary

3

suggests that careful consideration should be given to the social and economic problems represented by the proprietors of such shops having to abandon their way of life.

5   It seems likely that the number of shops will drop by about a fifth, from rather over 500,000 in 1966 to about 400,000 in 1980.

6   Multiples* are likely to increase their share of the total market greatly; this increase is likely to be almost wholly at the expense of independent retailers*.

7   The relative strength of independent retailers will depend on advantageous location, on specialisation, on the personal service they offer, and on the spread of voluntary groups.

8   There is likely to be a trend toward larger supermarkets. By 1980 we would estimate that about 400 supermarkets, each of over 10,000 square feet, will account for nearly 10 per cent of total food sales and will also sell an increasing quantity of non-food goods.

9   Most of these large supermarkets will be run by about half a dozen major supermarket chains, which will take a very large share of food sales in these and in their other branches. There will be several other smaller chains, largely regional, occupying mainly locations in secondary centres and emphasising the sale of fresh foods: co-operatives and independent supermarkets affiliated to voluntary groups will compete for much the same market.

10   Many more people will go shopping by car: one result of this will be that much more shopping will be carried out in the form of major weekly shopping expeditions (probably at the weekend) with a few supplementary trips in between. It seems likely that evening opening will be relatively limited, with shops being open on perhaps two nights a week until the mid-evening.

11   A number of factors connected with population, shop mix, centre design and centre management were isolated as contributing to the success or failure of shopping developments (see Chapter 5). The results of our enquiries, and the number of unsuccessful centres discovered where important principles have been disregarded, emphasise the great attention that needs to be paid to these factors. Both public authorities and private developers should provide themselves with greater resources and expertise than have hitherto been drawn on, in order to assess proposed developments. We also conclude that there is a need for more organised study of these factors (see recommendation 4).

12   It seems unlikely that central business areas of major towns will lose their importance as shopping centres: their share of total trade will probably remain about the same. However, planned shopping centres* in suburban areas are likely to account for an increasing proportion of total turnover, at the expense of other, more marginal, locations, such as 'street-corner' shops and areas adjacent to town centres. The share of trade which might be taken by free-standing superstores* (such as the Woolco development at Oadby) and by regional out-of-town shopping centres* (such as the centre which

* See Glossary

4

was proposed at Haydock Park) will depend on the attitude of central government and local authorities, both in positive planning and in reaction to developers' proposals.

Recommendations   We make the following recommendations:

1   Strategies adopted with regard to shopping provision in coming years must take account of the fact that given present trends there is every indication that either the gross rate of new building will have to be cut back or that the rate of obsolescence will increase. There is no likelihood of the return of a 'seller's market' for new developments. This requires that particular attention should be given to the factors we have identified as leading to success or failure when applications for new developments are considered.

2   In order to plan shopping provision rationally, planning must be done over wide enough areas to enable strategic plans to be drawn up on a regional basis: this is essential in view of the hierarchical nature of the pattern of shopping centres in this country. The Town and Country Planning Act of 1968 lays on each planning authority the duty of preparing a structure plan, and we would hope that the new procedure will result in such a regional strategy being applied.

3   Any fundamental large scale examination of the problems of shopping provision is necessarily hampered to a disabling extent by the absence of accurate and suitably disaggregated data about existing floorspace. The gathering of such data should be given a high priority in the forthcoming Census of Distribution for 1971. In the longer term, consideration should be given to the possibility of using the Inland Revenue data on floorspace (which is at present made available only to the Department of the Environment) for the purpose of providing information on floorspace in future censuses. Data on floorspace in Scotland and Northern Ireland should be similarly centralised and made available.

4   In view of our finding regarding the importance of the various factors which influence the success or failure of shopping centres, and in view of the lack of any body co-ordinating current studies, we recommend that serious consideration should be given to the setting up of such a body, possibly along the lines of the Institute for Centre Planning in Denmark, which draws most of its funds from consultancy fees; the Institute received a government grant in its early years but is now able to operate without one.

5   Some of the most serious problems affecting shopping developments in town centres arise from the increasing use of the car. While we recognise that in many respects public transport is unlikely to compete with the car for convenience, the sub-committee regards the maintenance of effective public transport as a matter of great importance.

6   We would regard it as essential not to underestimate future car parking requirements for both new developments and existing facilities. There is some evidence that in this country the standards envisaged for 1980 are about the same as those already adopted on the Continent. We would regard these standards as likely to be

quite insufficient ten years fron now, by which time the number of private cars will have doubled.

7   We consider it desirable that the policy of converting existing shopping streets for use by pedestrians only should be pursued more vigorously. Pedestrian areas must be well served by parking facilities and by public transport, and must also have adequate facilities for the receipt and despatch of goods. While there may be difficulties in individual locations, and each must be considered on its merits, we would regard the resistance sometimes offered by retailers to pedestrianisation as generally unjustified.

8   We have noted the considerable development in North America and in Europe of free standing superstores and of 'out-of-town' regional shopping centres. There are very few developments of the first kind in this country and none of the latter on any significant scale. Rightly or wrongly, the impression is widely held that both central government and local planning authorities hold an adverse attitude to them. We recognise that in both cases telling arguments have been adduced both for and against their development in this country, and we have not been able to arrive at a unanimous view regarding them. However, because of the importance of these kinds of development in countries having comparable standards of living, we consider it highly desirable that the Department of the Environment should lay down guide lines stating criteria for their acceptability: such guidance, based on analysis of the financial and social costs involved, would be of great help to all those concerned with developing a high standard of shopping provision.

9   As shopping habits change and as the ways of going shopping change, greater flexibility and freedom to experiment in respect of opening hours should be encouraged. Such experiments could lead to a greater utilisation of existing shopping capacity. We would recommend that this point needs closer study.

10   We consider the provision of a high standard of amenities in shopping centres to be very important. The provision of such amenities as play areas, seats, public lavatories and an attractive setting are of great importance to shoppers in creating a comfortable place to shop in. We would draw particular attention to the need to cater for the infirm and disabled in the design of shopping centres.

Chapter 3 Floorspace requirements in 1980

In order to estimate how floorspace requirements are likely to change it is necessary to consider:

1　How the total amount of consumers' spending in shops may change: this is examined in the first section of this chapter.

2　How the intensity of use of floorspace, as measured in sales per square foot, is likely to change: this is examined in the second section, which is prefaced by a review of the data available on the subject of sales per square foot.

The chapter concludes with a calculation of the floorspace likely to be required, given the information available. It should be stressed that our conclusions rest on a number of assumptions, especially that present trends will continue. While we consider that on the whole this assumption is reasonably realistic, it must be noted that any significant alteration of present trends would affect our conclusions.

Changes in consumer spending in shops

Consumer expenditure in 1980 was estimated by the Department of Applied Economics at Cambridge, details of the method used being summarised in Appendix D. Three sets of differing assumptions were used:

1　Gross domestic product would increase at either
(a)　a high growth rate of 3.75 per cent pa or
(b)　a low growth rate of 2.75 per cent pa.

2　Food prices would either
(a)　remain in the same proportion to those of non-food goods as now or
(b)　increase by 15 per cent as a result of entry into the Common Market.

3　In the case of assumption 2(b)
(a)　money incomes would remain constant, or
(b)　real incomes would remain constant.

While these assumptions were made explicitly, it should also be noted that there was an important implicit assumption inherent in the structure of the model, namely that economic conditions would show such stability that extrapolations could meaningfully be made from the 1950s and 1960s forward to 1980. This was particularly important in view of the fact that the base years were years of full employment. There have been suggestions that a policy of stringent control of the supply of money will inevitably lead to a much higher level of unemployment. This might well in its turn imply considerable changes in the shape of the distribution of earnings and hence of the distribution of individual spending power. We do not know

Table 1   Consumers' expenditure in shops, 1960, 1969 and 1980, £m 1963 prices

	1960		1969		1980 2.75% growth in GDP						1980 3.75% growth in GDP					
					Basic food price		Real incomes constant (Food price up 15%)		Money incomes constant (Food price up 15%)		Basic food price		Real incomes constant (Food price up 15%)		Money incomes constant (Food price up 15%)	
	£m	%	£m	%	£m	%	£m	%	£m	%	£m	%	£m	%	£m	%
Food, drink, tobacco	5,494	55.7	6,031	53.8	7,126	50.1	6,999	49.5	6,816	49.5	7,446	48.7	7,297	48.0	7,213	48.4
Clothing and footwear	1,761	17.9	2,123	18.9	2,809	19.7	2,826	19.9	2,756	20.1	3,067	20.0	3,087	20.3	3,014	20.2
Furniture	453	4.6	474	4.2	738	5.2	738	5.2	721	5.2	828	5.4	828	5.5	804	5.4
Radio/TV/electrical	404	4.1	503	4.5	828	5.8	828	5.9	798	5.8	953	6.2	953	6.3	917	6.2
Miscellaneous household goods	1,740	17.7	2,084	18.6	2,736	19.2	2,754	19.5	2,680	19.5	3,008	19.6	3,029	19.9	2,952	19.8
Total retail expenditure	9,858	100	11,215	100	14,237	100	14,145	100	13,771	100	15,302	100	15,191	100	14,900	100
Less mail order	299		449		712		707		688		765		759		745	
Total expenditure in shops	9,559		10,766		13,525		13,438		13,083		14,537		14,432		14,245	

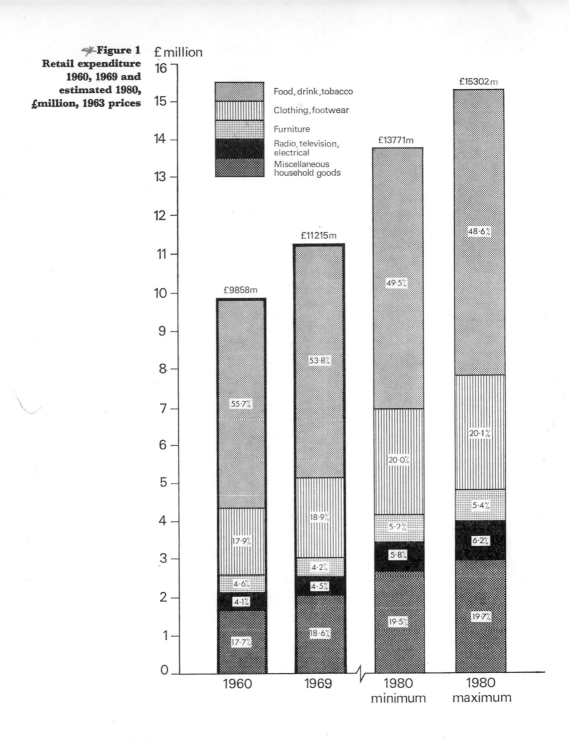

**Figure 1
Retail expenditure
1960, 1969 and
estimated 1980,
£million, 1963 prices**

£ million

Food, drink, tobacco
Clothing, footwear
Furniture
Radio, television, electrical
Miscellaneous household goods

£9858m

55·7%

17·9%

4·6%

4·1%

17·7%

£11215m

53·8%

18·9%

4·2%

4·5%

18·6%

£13771m

49·5%

20·0%

5·2%

5·8%

19·5%

£15302m

48·6%

20·1%

5·4%

6·2%

19·7%

1960

1969

1980
minimum

1980
maximum

what is actually going to happen, but historical data[1] do suggest that the dispersion (measured in percentage terms) of earnings has changed remarkably little from 1886 to the present day. Nevertheless, it should be stressed that this assumption of no significant change from past conditions is being made.

Tables showing estimates of consumers' expenditure as a whole for the years 1975 and 1980 are given in Appendix D. For the purpose of this chapter we are concerned only with consumers' expenditure in shops, and our estimate of this is shown in Figure 1 and in Table 1.

Since we are primarily concerned with limiting cases and an expected or mean value, further calculations are based on a high extreme of 14,500 million, a low extreme of 13,100 million and a mean value of 13,800 million.

In assessing shopping needs it is also necessary to consider shifts in the general pattern of spending, and in Appendix D we compare the percentages of consumers' expenditure anticipated for different commodity groups with those obtaining in 1968. Our figures suggest that the proportion of income spent on furniture will rise slightly, and on clothing, radio, television and electrical goods quite significantly; there will also be marked rises in expenditure on housing and cars. But the proportion of income spent on food will fall significantly and that spent on miscellaneous household goods will remain about the same. A consideration of the income and expenditure elasticities of the several commodity groups (see Appendix D) suggests a similar conclusion.

Floorspace utilisation – review of data

The available data on floorspace are extremely unsatisfactory. What is needed before any definite conclusions can be drawn is a comprehensive review of shop floorspace over the whole country broken down by:

1 Local authority areas
2 Location (ie central shopping area as against suburban locations at the very least)
3 Trade type
4 Turnover of shop
5 Organisational type of shop.

At present the only comprehensive figures on floorspace are those issued by the Ministry of Housing and Local Government (now the Department of the Environment) in 1969[2] [3]. These give figures of gross floorspace broken down by county boroughs and administrative counties, by Greater London boroughs and by statistical subdivisions of economic planning regions. They include banks in shopping areas and restaurants but exclude those assessed with living accommodation. There is no breakdown by smaller areas, trade type, location, turnover, or organisational type, and the analysis is limited to England and Wales.

The 1966 Census of Distribution collected floorspace data on a sample basis. Collection proved extremely difficult because of the non-co-operation of some respondents, and it is understood that the floorspace data ultimately published may be extremely limited. We would urge that the census authorities should make every effort to secure reliable figures in the full Census of 1971, as this appears to be the only opportunity in the near future to gather the information required in a way which will permit a breakdown in the manner outlined above. We understand that the ultimate intention may be to code the results of the Department of the Environment Enquiry (for which the figures are derived from the Inland Revenue) and of future Censuses of Distribution in such a way that the Department's figures can be processed to provide the necessary floorspace data in the Census. There are obvious administrative and practical obstacles, but we would urge that every effort should be made to overcome them, as it appears to be the only way in which suitably disaggregated floorspace figures (and hence figures on shop floor utilisation) can be obtained. This, however, must inevitably be some time in the future. In any case, no centralised records of shopping floorspace in Scotland exist at all.

At present the only data for local authority areas are those gathered by the local authorities for their own purposes, usually with the aim of assessing floorspace requirements in individual towns: such information is usually limited to the central shopping area, and may be gathered by the local authority staff themselves or by consultants. Enquiries made of local planning authorities in order to secure floorspace figures for the 167 towns with central shopping areas in the Census of Distribution of 1961 secured returns broken down between 'convenience' floorspace (food, confectionery and tobacco) and 'durable' floorspace (other shops) from 128 of them: a few others were able to supply floorspace figures which were not disaggregated. The figures were not all given on the same basis (most were nett, but some gross) and even where nett figures were given it was impossible to tell whether the criteria of measurement were identical in all cases. Further disaggregation by trade type was available in many instances, but not by any other cross-classification. Very little information is available for non-central areas of shopping floorspace.

Information on turnover per square foot by trade and organisational type was available only in a few instances. Some trade organisations (eg the Retail Distributors' Association and the National Federation of Ironmongers) made available figures disaggregated to a degree which is extremely useful: the coverage of such statistics is of course limited to their own members. For most trades such information is either not available or, where it exists, is regarded as highly confidential (this is especially the case with supermarket chains). A number of authors have produced estimates of turnover per square foot for individual trades (a summary is given in our report *Urban Models in Shopping Studies*[4]) but examination of these figures reveals very considerable variation in their estimates.

We therefore make the following recommendations:

Thought should be given to the collection of data on sales per square foot in different kinds of shop – both by shop type (butcher, baker etc) and by shop organisation (co-op, multiple etc). To some extent this has been done in the Census of Distribution for 1966, but this is only on a very limited sample basis and may well be little more than a useful pointer.

There is also need for more sophistication and disaggregation in the tables that are published. There is, for example, no breakdown between multiples, co-operative shops and independents of the sales figures for individual trades in the local tables. Obviously there are difficulties here regarding confidentiality, but it would have been extremely useful to have a breakdown between 'convenience' and 'durable' shops.

It would also be useful to have more than the means of the distributions of sales per square foot: the standard deviation or some other measure of dispersion would also be of interest, and, if not published, should be made available for consultation.

Rate of change of sales per square foot

In order to estimate the floorspace required in 1980 it is important to know the rate at which sales per square foot are changing in real terms (ie making allowance for the effect of inflation upon prices). To get an accurate idea of this it would be necessary to have the data from two full Censuses incorporating information on sales per square foot.

Since not even one is available, it is necessary to fall back on a method which is very much second best, but which does appear to give realistic results.

Estimates of the rate of change of sales per square foot were taken from as many published sources as were readily available. These fell into two groups:

1   Data supplied by trade associations (ie essentially *historical* data)
2   Estimates prepared by consultants, academics etc. While these were to some extent hypothetical, they were derived at one remove from information acquired from much the same sources as (1) although they would obviously be modified by individual circumstances.

These data suggested that the annual increase in the rate of floorspace utilisation is 1.0 per cent for 'convenience' shops, 1.5 per cent for 'durable' shops and 1.3 per cent for all shops. This conclusion is broadly confirmed by such studies of the subject as are available[5] [6]. The rate of change in floorspace utilisation might of course alter between now and 1980, and any significant change would naturally affect our conclusions. It can, however, be argued that such a change would require a technical breakthrough in retailing of a similar order to the introduction of self-service. No such breakthrough seems imminent or foreseeable at the moment, so the rate of increase in shop floor utilisation is here assumed to remain constant up to 1980.

Floorspace requirements in 1980

Details of the calculation of the floorspace required in 1980 are given in Appendix E. The conclusions are represented in Table 2.

In this table column 1 gives an estimate of the floorspace in each region and in England and Wales as a whole (no figures are available for Scotland and Northern Ireland).

Columns 2 to 4 give estimates of the floorspace required, given:

1   The estimates of spending in shops cited above, converted to spending per capita

Table 2 Floorspace in 1980

Region	1 Present floorspace (1968) (m sq ft)	2 Estimated floorspace required (m sq ft) Low	3 Middle	4 High	5 Extrapolated availability of floorspace (m sq ft)	6 % excess of extrapolated availability over estimated requirement Low	7 Middle	8 High
North	41.3	41.7	45.7	46.3	47.4	+ 13.8	+ 8.8	+ 2.2
Yorkshire/Humberside	57.4	58.0	61.4	64.9	70.0	+ 20.7	+ 14.0	+ 8.9
North West	83.1	83.9	88.9	94.9	92.2	+ 10.0	+ 3.7	— 1.9
East Midlands	34.8	38.2	40.4	42.5	43.2	+ 13.0	+ 6.9	+ 1.3
West Midlands	51.1	53.6	57.2	60.3	66.4	+ 23.9	+ 16.0	+ 10.0
East Anglia	17.9	22.1	23.3	24.5	21.6	— 2.3	— 7.3	— 11.9
South East	206.6	212.8	225.2	237.6	247.9	+ 16.4	+ 10.1	+ 4.2
South West	44.1	47.2	49.8	52.5	55.1	+ 16.8	+ 10.3	+ 5.0
Wales	28.1	28.4	29.8	31.5	32.3	+ 13.8	+ 8.3	+ 2.6
Total England and Wales	564.4	585.9	621.7	655.0	676.1	+ 15.4	+ 8.8	+ 3.2

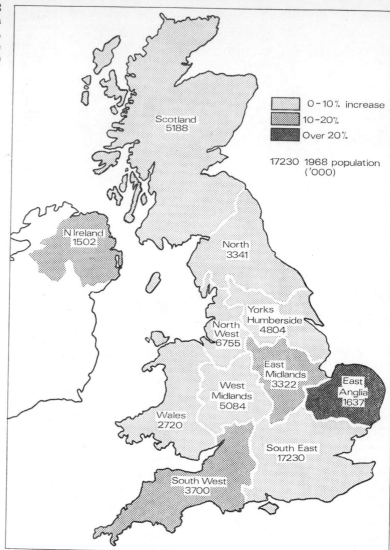

Figure 2
1968 UK population
by economic planning regions,
with estimated percentage
increase in population by 1980

Scotland
5188

N Ireland
1502

North
3341

Yorks
Humberside
4804

North
West
6755

East
Midlands
3322

East
Anglia
1637

West
Midlands
5084

Wales
2720

South East
17230

South West
3700

0-10% increase

10-20%

Over 20%

17230 1968 population
('000)

14

2 The estimate of the rate of change of shop floor utilisation given above

3 The Registrar-General's estimates of population for 1980 (see Figure 2).

'Low', 'middle' and 'high' estimates are given, to correspond with the different estimates of the amount spent in shops using different assumptions about national economic growth and the relative movement of food prices.

Column 5 of Table 2 gives an estimate of the floorspace which would be available given a continuation of the rate of nett building which obtained in the years 1964–67[2]; we have no material for calculating what actually will be built in the next ten years, and this is the only assumption we can make on a quantitative basis. These figures were calculated for each region and for the country as a whole.

Columns 6, 7 and 8 show the percentage differences between column 5 (extrapolated floorspace) and columns 2, 3 and 4 (required floorspace) respectively. A positive difference does not necessarily mean an excess of floorspace represented by empty shops, new or old. It is far more likely to mean either that:

1 New construction will be cut back, or

2 Shops in marginal locations will close or be converted to other uses at a greater rate than in recent years, or

3 A combination of these two processes.

Similarly, a negative difference does not suggest a deficit in floorspace so much as an acceleration of new construction, a deceleration in the rate of obsolescence, or both.

The general conclusion for the country as a whole is that new construction is likely to decline compared with 1964–67 or that the process of obsolescence will accelerate. This latter process will be especially significant in marginal areas. We examine these in more detail in Chapter 6, but the main locations where accelerated obsolescence will be significant are:

1 'Street-corner' shops

2 Areas on the periphery of central shopping areas: in fact there will be a tendency for central shopping areas to contract and be more intensively used (a process which is already visible in many towns).

The only area where new building will accelerate or obsolescence will be delayed is likely to be East Anglia, where the Registrar-General's forecast increase of population is much the greatest and there is a high incidence of new and expanded towns.

The sub-committee would have felt it desirable to disaggregate these figures in more detail, and in particular to examine the split between central shopping areas and other shopping areas: the data, however, did not permit this.

It would have been helpful if we could have calculated the desirable level of 'spare' shopping capacity and the optimal rate of obsolescence: neither the material nor the time for this were, unfortunately, available. These subjects could be studied with advantage.

References

1 A R Thatcher, 'The distribution of earnings of employers in Great Britain', *J R Statist Soc*, A, Vol 131 part 2, 1968

2 Ministry of Housing and Local Government, *Statistics for Town and Country Planning, Series II Floorspace,* No 1, HMSO, 1969

3 Ministry of Housing and Local Government, *Statistics for Town and Country Planning Series II Floorspace,* No 2, HMSO, 1969

4 Models Working Party, *Urban Models in Shopping Studies,* NEDO, 1970

5 T Rhodes and R Whitaker, 'Forecasting Shopping Demand', *Journal of the Town Planning Institute,* May 1967

6 South Bedfordshire Sub-regional Study Technical Committee, *Shopping Report* 1967

Chapter 4 Changing shopping patterns

Retailing involves the interaction of three parties: suppliers (ie manufacturers and wholesalers), retailers and shoppers. This report is mainly concerned with the way the latter groups behave: the behaviour of different kinds of retailer will depend on relative financial strength, and that of consumers will reflect increasing real income and leisure – but it must be emphasised that retailers and shoppers are interdependent.

The aim of this chapter is to examine the most important qualitative changes which will affect retailing between now and 1980; since these changes affect widely differing facets of the shopping scene the treatment is inevitably discursive. The sources of our observations are a survey we conducted among both retailers and other interested parties about the future pattern of retailing (see Appendix C), and the recently published Lintas survey[1]. We also draw, where this is relevant, on available evidence of trends in the United States and in Western Europe.

Number of shops In 1961 the number of shops in Great Britain was 542,000, and in 1966 504,000[2] (both figures exclude market traders and mobile shops). Respondents to our questionnaire anticipated a fall to 450,000 by 1975 and to 400,000 by 1980 (median figures). The reasons for this decline appear to be as follows:

1 Replacement of old shops by new ones is leading to a closure of businesses unable to pay the higher rents involved
2 Multiples and co-operative societies are rationalising their businesses, closing down smaller units and opening fewer, larger ones[3]
3 Competition from multiples is making it increasingly difficult for many independent traders to stay in business
4 The recent restrictions on credit have taken a larger toll on small shops
5 Large supermarkets and superstores, with a wide range of goods on offer, have led to increasingly large quantities of goods being handled by a comparatively small number of outlets.

A similar tendency towards reduction in the number of retail outlets may be observed both in Western Europe and the USA: there has been an absolute reduction in the number of retail establishments in every European country (with the exception of Italy, Spain and Portugal, countries in a different stage of development)[4], and between 1958 and 1963 the number of retail outlets in the USA fell by 6.4 per cent[5]. The decline has continued since the latter date.

Shares of trade of different types of organisation Respondents to the questionnaire were asked how they saw the market share of different types of outlet changing up to 1975, given

[handwritten margin note:] ie retailing organisations having ten or more brandes.

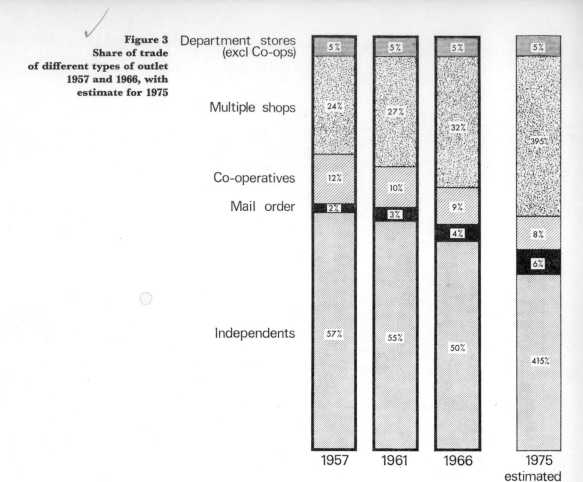

**Figure 3
Share of trade
of different types of outlet
1957 and 1966, with
estimate for 1975**

Department stores
(excl Co-ops)

Multiple shops

Co-operatives

Mail order

Independents

	1957	1961	1966	1975
Department stores (excl Co-ops)	5%	5%	5%	5%
Multiple shops	24%	27%	32%	39·5%
Co-operatives	12%	10%	9%	8%
Mail order	2%	3%	4%	6%
Independents	57%	55%	50%	41·5%

1957   1961   1966   1975
                        estimated

the Census figures from 1957 to 1966 (the respondent's median estimate is shown in the last column of figure 3). The trends indicated in figure 3 were envisaged as continuing up to 1980.

This block diagram tells us little about the changes which have in recent years been occurring in size, layout and retailing methods of shops, notably the replacement of many small counter shops by self-service units or large supermarkets. Such changes have often been taking place within the kind of organisation – eg multiples – and are therefore largely hidden within the figures on which the diagram is based.

Department stores   These were expected to maintain the same proportion of trade in 1975 and 1980. This implies that the ability to withstand the dynamic trading of the leading multiple shops, which has been shown in recent years, will continue. In particular, we would envisage a continued tendency to move to the suburbs and new centres of population.

In Europe there has been a continuous growth in the number and size of department stores. The number of department stores has increased from 500 in 1960 to 670 in 1970, and the selling space increased by 16 million square feet to 52 million square feet. In both cases, the shares of these forms of retailing in total retail trade rose in these years.

In the USA department stores have been one of the most dynamic sectors of retailing. Their number rose from 2,760 in 1954 to 4,250 in 1963, and their sales nearly doubled in the same period, rising from 10.6 billion dollars to 20.5 billion dollars (representing an increase in the share of total sales from 9.1 per cent to 12.5 per cent)[5*]. Important reasons for this dynamic change were the increase in the standard of living in the States and the policy of supplementing 'down-town' stores by stores in suburban and 'out-of-town' locations. (It has been suggested that in the UK some chains such as Marks and Spencers pre-empt part of the trade enjoyed by department stores abroad and that this limits the opportunities for the expansion of department stores in this country.)

Multiple shops   Respondents to the questionnaire foresaw a substantial increase in the share of total sales which would be made by multiples.

The greatly increased share of trade taken by multiples in the past few years suggests that they are in a strong position for continued expansion. The reason for this lies in the management resources on which they can draw, and in their ability to buy in large quantities and supply common services to their stores[6]. Because of their economies of operation and their ability to attract relatively high customer traffic, they can afford the higher rents in the new shopping developments, which many independents cannot, and they are also in a position to bargain for rent concessions, since their presence

---

* It should be noted that the US Census figures for retail trade include certain categories, such as farm equipment dealers, car dealers, petrol stations, and eating and drinking places, that do not come within the British Census of Distribution definition. In this chapter the figures have been adapted to allow for this, but some minor differences of categorisation still remain.

and reputation will help to draw customers to a new development.

A similar expansion in the share of total trade taken by multiples is to be seen both in Western Europe (where governmental policy in the inter-war years tended in some cases to place them under severe handicaps[4]) and in the USA, where between 1954 and 1967 the share of trade taken by multiples rose from 18 per cent to 27 per cent[5]).

Co-operative societies

Figure 3 indicates a continuing decline in co-operative societies' share of total retail trade between 1957 and 1966. Respondents to the questionnaire on the future pattern of retailing suggested a further drop to 8 per cent in 1975, stabilising at that level or just below it.

The performance of the co-operative societies in past years, judged from a purely financial point of view, has been inhibited by the fact that they have had to follow two aims which were in some ways hard to reconcile. On the one hand they had to behave as a multiple retailer (and collectively they form much the largest multiple chain); on the other they sought to fulfil their responsibilities as a consumers' co-operative responsible to its members. This induced both a conservative outlook and a tendency to provide services which were uneconomic from a commercial viewpoint.

The main faults of the organisation were pinpointed in the Gaitskell Report of 1958[7] but the action taken on this was slow. Since 1966, however, the pace of change in the movement has become much more rapid: to cite a few examples, there have been 'Operation Facelift', vigorous television advertising, a much more determined reduction in the number of societies, considerable rationalisation of sites, and in many cases the replacement of the old 'divi' by stamps. The movement has never been incapable of innovation (it introduced self-service during the war): its main difficulty has been getting rid of the old rather than introducing the new. False dawns have been heralded before, but there is evidence that the present organisational changes are going a long way towards stopping the slide in the co-op's market share – largely by making the movement behave more like any other multiple. (Whether this will affect the democratic nature of the movement it is impossible to say: this is largely the province of its political, welfare and educational aspects, which are outside the scope of this report.) Comparison with experience abroad is vitiated by the fact that co-operatives' share of total trade varies from nation to nation largely for historical reasons: eg in Sweden they take about a fifth of total trade, but in the USA very little.

Mail order

Respondents to the questionnaire suggested that general mail order houses' share of total trade would rise from 4 per cent in 1966 to 6 per cent by 1975 and rather more by 1980: we would, however, reject this: continental experience cited below suggests a ceiling of about 5 per cent.

'At one time the mail order business tended to be concentrated in the North and to be used by the working class only. In recent years it has spread to other parts of the country, while certain catalogues have been deliberately designed to appeal to a wider social spectrum, for example Norman Hartnell is fashion advisor to Great Universal Stores. There is undoubtedly scope for expanding the market further both geographically and up the social scale'.[1]

There might also be scope for extending the range of goods usually bought, which tends to be dominated by clothing and footwear (51 per cent), ironmongery (9 per cent) and fancy goods, sports goods and toys (7 per cent)[2].

The importance of this type of selling has increased in every European country in the past decade. The most spectacular increase in the post-war years has occurred in Germany where mail order selling now represents some 4.5 per cent of the total retail trade. In other continental European countries the share of this form of retailing is still below 2 per cent. But while the share of mail order selling in Germany has levelled off in the past three or four years, its share in trade in the other countries is still rising.

In America the share of total trade accounted for by mail order fell slightly between 1954 and 1963 from 3.9 per cent to 3.8 per cent[5].

Independent traders   The increase in market share held by multiples was seen by respondents to the questionnaire as being largely at the expense of independent traders, whose share was anticipated to fall to 41 per cent by 1975, with a further drop by 1980.

Small independent traders certainly have a place in the pattern of retailing, as has already been pointed out in the EDC's evidence to the Bolton Committee[8]. They are usually close to their customers, often operate flexible hours and offer the 'personal touch'. Often, too, they can offer specialised goods and services which would be uneconomic for multiples to offer.

But the factors leading to the reduction in numbers of shops – SET, high rental redevelopment, competition by multiples and supermarkets, and the squeeze – have affected the small independents, with their limited resources, more than any other sector. An examination of the confectionery, tobacco and newsagents' trades[9] (perhaps the trades 'par excellence' of the small independent) suggested that a major cause of falling numbers was a combination of lack of dynamism on the part of small shopkeepers and changes in shopping habits brought about by property redevelopment. Reference to lack of dynamism is significant, since if the small shopkeepers concerned were more dynamic they would presumably not remain *small* shopkeepers. Retailers under this kind of pressure are in fact those who are least capable of responding to it. For this reason alone a considerable number of closures in the independent sector is to be anticipated.

Respondents to our questionnaire were asked which factors were likely to be most significant in contributing to the survival of independents. Specialisation and personal service emerged as the two most important factors, followed by the growth of voluntary groups. Concentration on 'off-centre' locations and longer opening hours received far less support, although they are frequently mentioned in discussions of the subject. These conclusions are broadly supported by the Lintas survey[1]. No mention was made of collective department stores run by independent retailers, of which some 35 have been set up in Western Europe, with varying success.

Voluntary groups

Voluntary groups, which began growing rapidly about 10 years ago, accounted for 22.4 per cent of retail grocery turnover in October/ November 1969, reaching this level from 20 per cent the previous year. Of the two kinds of voluntary groups those run as retail buying groups in 1966 accounted for rather a larger number of both outlets and turnover than those run by wholesalers, although the latter are dominant among the food trades[1] [2]. This position may have changed since.

'With increasingly competitive promotional policies and keen prices (most have a wide range of own labels, and some comparatively large advertising budgets), added to the convenience of being near at hand, members of these groups are meeting a consumer need which should ensure for them a strong place in the 70s. They will continue in business because they are complementary to the multiples rather than directly competitive to them'[1].

The Distributive Trades EDC has encouraged the growth of voluntary groups.

'The EDC feels that the group principle is a valuable one since it makes it possible to combine the flexibility and independence of smaller units with the management techniques and advantages of scale of a larger organisation. At present voluntary groups occur mainly in distribution, but they may contain lessons for other sectors and there is no reason why the voluntary group principle should be limited to buying for resale. It is only fair to point out however that in order to compete successfully with larger firms, the voluntary groups have tended to become tightly-knit organisations and the independence of members has to some extent been reduced. There has also been a considerable degree of merging between firms in groups, particularly among wholesale members'[8].

Respondents to the questionnaire were asked in which trades (beside food) they thought voluntary groups were likely to develop most in the coming years. Hardware, pharmacy, electrical goods and textiles were regarded as the most important.

Share of food trade accounted for by different methods of selling

Response to the questionnaire on the future pattern of retailing showed that the share of total food trade taken by grocery* outlets would increase from 40 per cent in 1961 to 53 per cent in 1980: the sale of food in predominantly non-food shops (eg Woolworths and Marks and Spencer) was also likely to rise. Specialist food shops like butchers, bakers and green-grocers would drop from nearly 40 per cent in 1961 to 30 per cent in 1980. The share of total food trade by supermarkets* and superettes* would double to 26 per cent in 1980.

These figures indicate a fall in the share of trade held by specialist food shops and also (to a lesser degree) of non-supermarket grocery shops. Some authorities [1] [10] [11] see the main opportunity for these shops lying in concentration on fresh foods (bread, meat and fish, fruit, vegetables and dairy products) and also on the non-standard delicatessen lines which supermarkets might find it less profitable to handle.

This suggests that the small specialist store should concentrate on the fresh products the housewife is likely to be unable to keep, or that she may run out of, between major shopping expeditions, and a reduced emphasis on packaged and tinned goods. The Unigate report[10] showed, however that progress in this direction was depen-

* See Glossary

dent on improved methods of storage by wholesalers and delivery to small outlets.

Supermarkets   Probably by 1975 and certainly by 1980 there will be very few counter service shops of any size left in the grocery trade. The only grocery shops which will still offer counter service may be the very small ones of the 'corner shop' type which are too small or unprofitable to permit conversion and, possibly, a few larger ones in middle class areas which will continue to operate to meet the needs of those customers who like to be waited on. The grocery trade will become increasingly the province of the supermarkets.

Response to the questionnaire showed that the number of self-service grocery shops was expected to rise from 22,000 in 1966 to 28,000 in 1975 (this increase in numbers has in fact already taken place). Their share of grocery trade would rise from 57 per cent to 70 per cent in 1975, and of all food trade from 24 per cent now to 35 per cent in 1975. The bulk of this increase would not take place in the small self-service shops but in supermarkets of 2,000 sq ft upwards and especially in the largest supermarkets of 10,000 sq ft selling space. This last group is anticipated to quadruple in numbers to 400 by 1980, with the share of grocery trade rising from 4 per cent to 15 per cent and of all food trade from 2 per cent to 9 per cent.

In Europe there has been a rapid development of self-service selling and of supermarkets in the food trade. The number of self-service units in the countries of continental Europe increased from 38,000 in 1960 to 157,000 in 1970. And, much more important, the number of supermarkets, defined as self-service units with 4,000 sq ft of selling space or more, increased from 300 in 1960 to 5,750 in 1970. The average supermarket virtually replaces 10 to 15 traditional food shops, and the average size of the supermarket is growing every year.

America was a decade ahead of Europe in the development of supermarkets and while many new ones are being built, there are some signs of a levelling off in numbers[12][13]. The emphasis seems to be rather more than hitherto on remodelling and expansion of existing shops. Even so, the average size of new supermarkets is large, by British or European standards. The average new supermarket in 1968 measured 21,000 sq ft gross (15,000 sq ft nett).

The trend towards larger supermarkets implies that an increasing proportion of grocery and food trade will be taken by fewer and fewer shops. There seems to be strong grounds for thinking these shops will be in the hands of relatively few groups[14]. Table 3 summarises the standing of the principal supermarket chains at present, and illustrates especially the potential of the six largest groups.

There will also be competition from co-operative establishments (total turnover £750 million) and variety stores, for example Marks and Spencer (food turnover £86 million in 1969), Woolworths (£50 million) and British Home Stores (£12 million). In this regard it should be noted that most West European variety stores now include

Table 3

Turnover, total number of shops and number of supermarkets belonging to principal grocery companies

	£m turnover	Total shops	Of which supermarkets
Tesco Stores Ltd	238.4	774	444
Allied Suppliers Ltd	193.3	1,927	520
J Sainsbury Ltd	187.5	225	114
Fine Fare Ltd	153.0	1,087	510
International Stores Ltd	108.6	992	123
Moores Stores Ltd and Wrights Biscuits Ltd*	77.6	1,424	127
	958.4	6,429	1,838
Co-operative Retail Services Ltd	48.2	787	125
MacFisheries Ltd	42.6	356	44
London Co-op Soc Ltd	38.3	707	92
Key Markets Ltd	36.0	206	88
Associated Dairies Ltd†	34.3	120	19
Pricerite Ltd	29.2	107	93
Bishops Stores Ltd†	28.0	62	34
Unigate Ltd	24.4	508	44
Royal Arsenal Co-op Soc Ltd	24.3	423	42
David Greig Ltd	23.5	160	27
Waitrose Ltd	22.7	31	31
W Jackson & Son Ltd	20.0	69	29
Safeway Ltd	20.0	32	32
Birmingham Co-op Soc Ltd	16.1	332	22
Cater Brothers Ltd	15.6	35	9

* The two companies have interlocking boards
† Sales of the group
Source: IFD *Directory* [15]. Turnover figures are quoted for the last available year, in almost all cases a financial year ending during 1969 or 1970.

a food supermarket of at least 4,000 square feet. Such stores in this country are trading in the same way to an increasing extent.

Shares of non-food sales accounted for by different methods of selling

The general consensus of respondents to our questionnaire was that the share of the market held by specialist non-food shops would fall steadily from 75 per cent to rather over 65 per cent (for the reasons advanced above it is likely that the independent specialists will suffer most), that the share held by department and variety stores would increase from 25 per cent to 28 per cent, and that the share held by food shops would rise from 2 per cent to $6\frac{1}{2}$ per cent, the bulk of this being sold in the very large supermarkets which are now being built. Since the share of total trade held by department stores is envisaged as constant, this means that variety stores and supermarkets will make inroads into the trade held by 'specialist' shops.

Apart from this, the most important likely trend appears to be continued growth of multiples at the expense of independents, with possibly some casualties among the smaller multiples.

Markets

Surveys of retailing sometimes make no reference to markets, which is unfortunate because even though their share of the total trade is under 1 per cent, in some trades it is much more significant. Many markets continue to thrive, both of the typical 'fruit and vegetable' kind and those offering wider ranges of food and durable goods. The markets at Derby, for instance, account for a sizeable proportion of the trade of the town, and offer an extremely wide range and choice of goods. The drawing power of markets has been realised by many developers (eg at Walsall and Preston), and most new town development corporations have made provision for at least a small market. While the total share of trade is likely to remain very small overall, they are likely to continue to take a significant part of trade in fruit and vegetables and possibly other fresh foods, and to act as powerful magnets determining the routes taken by shoppers (and hence influencing the siting of shops).

New types of retailing

Respondents to the questionnaire were asked to estimate the future importance of automatic vending machines, punched card retailing*, telephone ordering and private customers shopping in cash and carry warehouses. The last technique was regarded as most important, followed at a distance by telephone ordering. Automatic vending came third (possibly because the question was asked with regard to its *general* importance: it is clearly likely to be of great importance for *particular* kinds of articles). Punched card retailing had little support and experiments in this made abroad have all failed so far (one would suspect that if 'the provision of food can be one of the most emotional areas in a woman's life'[16] this method of purchasing may be too impersonal).

Respondents thought that cash and carry was most important especially for food, but also for non-food. But it has been suggested[1] that by 1980 this form of buying will not account for a very substantial part of consumer spending because it is doubtful if the necessary conditions (access to warehouses, room to store provisions at home, availability of deep freezes in the home, non-servicing of durable items and, last but not least, economy-orientation as opposed to satisfaction-orientation) would obtain to a sufficient degree to make any significant difference to the general pattern of shopping.

Changes in patterns of consumer behaviour
When consumers will buy

Assuming a relaxation of present legal requirements, respondents were asked what changes they would expect by 1980 in the opening hours of (a) supermarkets, (b) other food shops, (c) non-food shops.

The general consensus was that any relaxation would take the form of opening at least some evenings per week rather than of seven-day opening, although there was a substantial minority that anticipated seven-day opening of supermarkets and, to a lesser extent, of food shops (but not non-food shops).

When asked when people actually would shop, however, the great majority suggested that people would shop at weekends (whether this would include Sunday or not would depend on legislation). Only a small minority thought people actually would

---

* See Glossary

shop in the evenings – an interesting conclusion when considered together with that in the previous paragraph, and one which suggests that late night opening would not in fact be attractive to shoppers in general. There is, in fact, some evidence that evening shopping is not particularly popular. A survey conducted in 1966 by Southern Television[17] showed that 82 per cent of shoppers never made use of late night opening, even though only 13 per cent said that there was no late night shopping in convenient reach. Even among supermarket users 73 per cent said that they never used this facility. But because more married women are going out to work and will want to fit in their shopping before or after work, it seems likely some shops in some locations will extend their opening hours to some extent, and that there will be at least one really late general extension (probably on Fridays). There does not seem much likelihood that shops will generally find it profitable to stay open late every night of the week, nor does it seem likely that Sunday opening will become general, although here again some shops will probably find it worthwhile to open. What does seem important is that there should be flexibility and freedom to experiment, as suggested by the Prices and Incomes Board[18], and it is impossible to ignore the trend towards extended evening and Sunday opening which has been apparent both in North America and in Western Europe[19]. This subject needs further study.

Number of shopping trips

Estimates of the average numbers of grocery shopping trips made by a housewife vary between two and four times per week[10 11 17 20]. The number of trips is dependent above all on the size of the family[17]. The available evidence seems to suggest that in the case of families with cars the tendency is to undertake one major shopping trip, mainly at weekends: in this case additional trips are to 'top up' supplies. The number of housewives having to shop on foot, using public transport, is diminishing: this means that the limitation on a shopping load is no longer what one woman can carry.

The weekly shopping trip (with minor 'topping up' expeditions in between) seems likely to be the pattern of the future. The limitation is no longer the capacity of the shopping basket but that of the car boot or, for certain goods, the refrigerator.

What is of interest is perhaps whether the main shopping trip will take place at intervals longer than a week. This would entail the use of a deep freezer. That the use of deep freezers will increase seems certain, but the rate of increase seems likely to depend on the rate of building new houses, since those existing in many cases lack the space to accommodate any but the smallest range of freezers.

One-stop shopping

A recent survey[11] has shown that 'one-stop shopping' is far from being current practice in this country. Most housewives visit two or three food shops on their main shopping trip, and supermarkets seem to have little impact in this respect. For both those who use supermarkets and those who do not, the norm is 'two and a half stop shopping' on main trips, and 'two stop shopping' on other trips – less than before the great growth of supermarkets in the last decade, but not as low as was generally expected at the beginning of this growth. Many shoppers on their main trip visit a butcher and a greengrocer as well: this may indicate dissatisfaction with the standard of meat, fruit and vegetables in supermarkets, but may equally be some evidence of innate resistance to the idea of doing all shopping under one roof.

Enjoying shopping   One last point: a recent survey[11] suggests that for most housewives the satisfaction of shopping derives from the actual enjoyment of the goods when they are brought home. There seems to be relatively little *enjoyment* of shopping as a social activity. This surely represents a challenge to retailers, developers and planners alike.

for out-of-town

References

[1] J Tanburn, *People, Shops and the '70s*, Lintas Special Projects 1970

[2] Board of Trade, *Censuses of Distribution* 1957, 1961, 1966, HMSO

[3] W B Reddaway, *Effects of the Selective Employment Tax. First Report on the Distributive Trades*, HMSO, 1970

[4] J B Jefferys and D Knee, *Retailing in Europe*, Macmillan, 1962

[5] US Bureau of the Census, *Statistical Abstract of the United States*, 1968 (89th edition) Washington DC, 1968

[6] National Board for Prices and Incomes, Report No 80, *Distributors' Margins on Paint, Children's Clothing, Household Textiles and Proprietary Medicines*, Cmd 3737, HMSO, 1968

[7] Co-operative Independent Commission Report, 1958

[8] Distributive Trades Little Neddy, *Special Report, Evidence to the Bolton Committee of Inquiry on Small Firms*, NEDO, 1970

[9] System Three, *Report of a Study of Confectioners, Tobacconists and Newsagents*, unpublished 1970

[10] Unigate Foods Ltd, *A Fresh Look for the Seventies*, May 1970

[11] British Market Research Bureau Ltd, *Shopping in the Seventies*, IPC Women's Weeklies, 1970

[12] Supermarket Institute, 21st Annual Report, *The Supermarket Industry Speaks 1969*

[13] Supermarket Institute, *Facts about New Supermarkets opened in 1968*, 1969

[14] K Van Musschenbroek, The Vigour of the Second Division, *Financial Times*, 5 November 1969

[15] Institute of Food Distribution, *Directory 1970*

[16] J Tanburn, *Food, Women and Shops*, Lintas Special Projects 1968

[17] Southern Independent Television, *The Southern Shopper Revisited*, 1966

[18] National Board for Prices and Incomes, Report No 97, *Distributors' Costs and Margins on Furniture, Domestic Electrical Appliances and Footwear*, Cmnd 3858, HMSO, 1968

[19] A H Bienfait, 'Late Closing Hours as a Helper to the Problem' paper given to 2nd international congress *Urbanisme et Commerce*, Stockholm, 1969

[20] Alfred Bird, 'Mrs Housewife and her Grocer', 1966, quoted in J Tanburn *People, Shops and the '70s*, Lintas Special Projects 1970

Chapter 5 Factors leading to the success or failure of shopping centres

If economic use is to be made of the resources applied to the provision of shopping floorspace, an understanding of what makes new shopping developments succeed or fail is highly desirable. Plainly, erection of a shopping precinct which attracts few tenants is wasteful: it involves a drain on the finances of developer and local authority alike, and usually on the few retailers who may set up in the development as well. A mistake of this nature can last for a long time, since building materials are durable, and may cause blight in the locality such as to induce indirect waste of resources.

But waste of resources does not only occur in the 'white elephants' – empty or poorly filled developments scattered up and down the country with their empty shells and boarded fronts standing as a monument to somebody's dreams or mistaken analysis. Even when the shops are filled, and customers are drawn in, there may be a waste of resources, albeit of a more subtle and less easily quantifiable kind.

Factors affecting success or failure may be of three basic kinds:

1   Purely commercial factors; examples are the construction of a development on the basis of incorrect analysis of the surrounding population's size or shopping habits, or design faults such as failure to realise the importance of a correct pedestrian flow, or failure to provide the right kind of storage or access facilities.

2   Amenity factors which can have an effect on the commercial performance of a centre, such as the neighbourhood of tower blocks creating air turbulence.

3   Amenity factors which may not affect a centre's commercial performance but which affect the people shopping there or the community at large: examples of these are the provision of seats or toilets and the whole range of aesthetic factors.

This chapter deals mainly with the first two kinds of factors, which bear directly or indirectly on commercial success. However, this is not to belittle the importance of amenity factors affecting the community, which will be discussed at the end of the chapter. The text deals mainly either with completely new shopping centres (eg those in new towns, or new developments such as the district centre at Cowley) or with substantial developments built in the last ten years in existing towns (such as the Bull Ring at Birmingham or the St George's centre at Preston): some of the comments are, however, applicable to existing shopping centres.

The conclusions stated in the following pages are based mainly on the results of research undertaken directly by the sub-committee or under its auspices; a description of the various projects undertaken is given in Appendix F.

The several surveys did not produce identical answers – the methodologies differed, and the sample populations were very different – but the following factors were isolated as being critical to the success or failure of a centre.

1   Population characteristics (eg number, income, socio-economic classification and shopping habits)

2   Factors connected with the composition of a centre:
(a)   Variety of shops
(b)   Presence and siting of 'magnets'

3   Factors connected with access:
(a)   Parking facilities
(b)   Public transport
(c)   Integration with existing pedestrian routes
(d)   Visibility of centre from a main street

4   Factors connected with centre design:
(a)   Absence of traffic
(b)   Weather protection
(c)   Number of levels
(d)   Pedestrian flow within the centre
(e)   Good design of individual shops,
        including:
        (i)   Adequate rear access
        (ii)   Adequate storage space
        (iii) Flexibility

5   Factors connected with the running of the centre:
(a)   Traders' associations and publicity
(b)   Leasing practice
(c)   Amenities

Population characteristics   It is vital that a centre should meet the requirements of the surrounding population. The calculation of these involves for the most part the construction of mathematical models, which are examined in detail in the report of the Sub-Committee's Models Working Group[1] in which will be found a bibliography of many of the principal methods used. (See also Jones[2].) Income level and socio-economic structure, the length of time people have lived in the neighbourhood, and the shopping habits of the population all need to be studied in detail in addition to the actual numbers in the dependent areas.

Mistakes have been made over the numbers of the dependent population. The Seacroft centre in Leeds is a case in point. A study of this centre[3] has shown that the planning authority in this case made an exaggerated estimate of the numbers who could be drawn to the centre. There was a large population within two to three miles, but the proximity of Leeds City Centre and the Crossgates centre made it necessary that in order to succeed Seacroft would need to be an extremely attractive centre in all ways: this was not the case.

An example where estimation of spending power proved incorrect was found at Doncaster. Only one projection was made for retail sales in the area in 1971. For this project a 4 per cent growth in the gross national product was assumed for the period 1963–71. This was admittedly in line with government forecasts at the time but no such growth rate was even remotely approached, and Doncaster's comparatively poorly favoured position, together with the running down of coal mines and railway workshops, meant that consumer spending fell far short of what was estimated. Perhaps some of the factors causing this could not have been foreseen, but the planners concerned could have given greater consideration to what would be the situation if the gross national product failed to grow in the way they envisaged, and could have taken into account the particular economic circumstances of the locality.

Social habits must also be borne in mind. Seacroft was very well served by buses but the population of surrounding estates, who had been transferred from the centre of Leeds in slum clearance programmes, persisted in returning to the city centre where they were used to shopping. Similarly, the population of Leigh Park, also moved several miles from Portsmouth by slum clearance programmes, for many years kept returning to the city centre for their weekly groceries; this held back the development of the Leigh Park shopping centre to a marked extent.

The correct assessment of a shopping centre's dependent population in respect of size and behavioural characteristics is vital. An error in this regard cannot be put right, and it is disturbing to find that large centres have been built in the recent past where either incorrect assumptions were made or where the analytical work was negligible or non-existent. An example of a study covering a wide region where particular attention was paid to the calculation of dependent shopping populations and the delineation of dependent areas may be found in the Haydock Park study[4]. (See Figure 4.)

Variety of shops This was cited as being of major importance in all surveys. That a wide range of shop types is a factor leading to success seems intuitively obvious and certainly the only centres which did not have a reasonably full range were markedly unsuccessful ones (Main centre, Derby and Waterdale, Doncaster). Even if variety of shops did not cause success, it was plainly concomitant with it.

But, counting up the number of Census of Distribution shop types, some of the less successful centres (eg Redhill) still had a wide range of shops, having even more types represented than some of the more successful ones. What seems to be essential is not only the presence of a given type of shop, but a comprehensive range of merchandise, competition and variety within that type: this applies especially to shops selling shoes or women's clothing (goods for which the 'comparison' element in shopping is very important). It is not difficult to find a location with six or more shoe shops in close proximity, but they each tend to place a slightly different emphasis on their wares; the same applies to clothing shops. The evidence of the pavement surveys of shoppers' opinions confirmed the attitude of multiple retailers interviewed, namely that a satisfactory variety of shops meant not only a good range of shop types and the mingling of multiple and independent, but variety of quality, price and target appeal. The juxtaposition of Tesco and Sainsbury usually benefits both; good provision of women's clothing shops requires the pro-

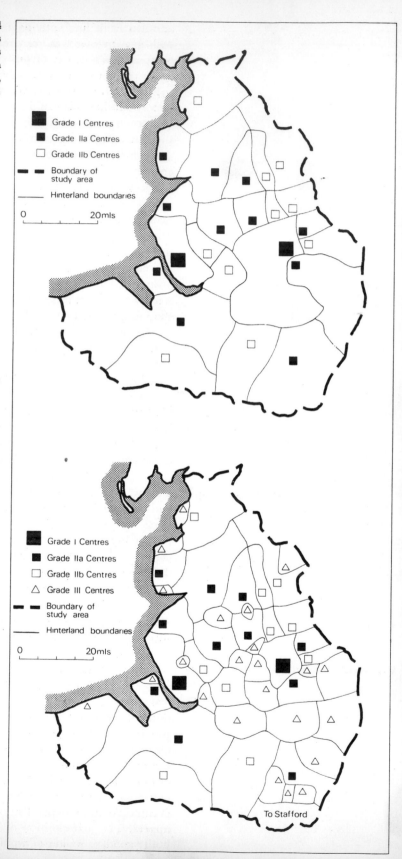

Figure 4
Dependent areas
for Grade II and Grade III towns
in the North West, as shown
by the Haydock Study Team,
University of Manchester, in 1961

Grade I Centres
Grade IIa Centres
Grade IIb Centres
Boundary of study area
Hinterland boundaries

0   20mls

Dependent areas of
Grade II towns

Grade I Centres
Grade IIa Centres
Grade IIb Centres
Grade III Centres
Boundary of study area
Hinterland boundaries

0   20mls

To Stafford

Dependent areas of
Grade III towns

vision of shops having appeal to widely varying ages and outlooks, from the 'dolly girl' to the old age pensioner. Cowley and Redhill were especially criticised for their lack of women's clothing shops. Both in fact have such shops but in each case they tend to appeal to a comparatively limited range of customers – and even these, one suspects, would welcome a wider choice of outlets. One of the ways women show their individuality is in their choice of clothes, and it is impossible to be certain of having the 'right thing' if the purchaser has only been able to go into one shop. The Basildon survey[5] brought out clearly the desire of consumers for 'specialist' and 'class' shops. The provision of shops which they considered purely utilitarian was plainly insufficient. The best known example of many shops stocking a comparatively narrow range of goods but offering a wide variety within that range is Carnaby Street in London. Such specialisation of location is, however, only likely to be found in a very large shopping centre.

Both private developers and development corporations emphasised the vital importance of deciding the tenant mix (which in many cases will involve deciding the identity of the tenants) at a very early stage, preferably even before the first brick is laid. One of the most successful operators said that advertising shops in the trade press was a confession of failure. The presence of a large buying population can never guarantee success in itself, but this can be effected by good tenant mix. Failure to get the tenant mix right at the beginning may result in a shopping centre having to admit non-retailing uses such as estate agents, insurance companies, army recruiting offices and the like, or even, as at Waterdale (Doncaster) betting shops and automatic bingo saloons. Whether or not such uses are individually desirable from a general social point of view, the surveys conducted suggested that the presence of such uses is a mark of an unsuccessful new location or a declining old one. Support for the deterrent effect of non-retail uses is provided by the Multiple Shops Federation[6], which suggested that shop windows should not be separated by the premises of those commercial services such as banks, estate agents and post offices, which are not dependent on window display. Such tenants are by no means undesirable in themselves: the most acceptable way of fitting them in is to fit them into a separate section away from the main shopping flow, as at Cowley and Hemel Hempstead, or to site them in first-floor offices.

Presence and siting of 'magnets'

'Magnets' – department stores and the major multiples (of which Marks and Spencer, Woolworths, Littlewoods, British Home Stores, C & A, Sainsburys and Tesco were regarded as the most important) were regarded as essential: without these, a development will have very limited drawing power compared with a nearby one where they are present (as may be seen by comparing the Arndale and Waterdale developments at Doncaster, and the Seacroft and Crossgates Centres at Leeds). The presence or absence of such magnets is a reflection of the developer's skill in providing a good site and good design and in assessing the population characteristics of the area correctly.

The siting of magnets can be crucial in determining the success of other shops in the centre, since they will determine the pedestrian flow within the centre. Current North American practice[7] is to site department stores at opposite ends of the main shopping mall as at Yorkdale (see photograph). Some of the latest centres in this country (eg the Victoria centre under construction at Nottingham) adopt a similar approach.

An example of the skilful siting of a magnet is the department store in the new development at Solihull, which helps to draw pedestrians off the main street and through the precinct.

Seacroft at Leeds illustrates the need for careful siting of magnets. This precinct is roughly cruciform, and the key tenants (Thrift, the Co-operative Society and Woolworths) were grouped together at the point where the arms of the cross met. As a result, the development is too centripetal, so that the wings to the north, south and west were never fully let, and the shops that did open there generally either failed or stagnated.

Normally more than one key tenant is necessary to ensure movement within a precinct: in one American centre 92 per cent of the centre's customers were at one time or another in the centre's one department store, but of this percentage 31 per cent were found to have entered and left directly from the car park[8]. For this reason a department store or supermarket by itself could not be relied on to promote movement within a centre.

In addition to the 'magnets', secondary attractors (ie those tenants whose trade is not dependent so much on location, such as groups of clothing shops) have an important part to play: by judicious siting of secondary attractors, shoppers can be induced to cross malls or squares to shop locations not directly on the main routes generated by the key tenants[2].

Left to themselves, the secondary attractors would probably tend to congregate round the principal magnets: such clustering may be seen in the high street of almost any town, and the desire for it was certainly encountered by the new town authorities in their early years (for example at Stevenage and Basildon). The evidence available suggests, however, that by now the major developers are fully aware of the importance of dispersing magnets and secondary attractors in such a way as to promote an optimal pedestrian flow past all shops in the centre.

Parking facilities   The need for adequate parking these days is obvious, and was given first priority in all our surveys. That parking has until lately been inadequate for present-day needs is shown by a comparison of the figures in Table 4 (page 53) (showing parking provision standards of county boroughs in 1966) with Table B5 (page 92) (showing parking provision standards in continental countries). The provision in new continental centres is at least 5.5 car park places per 1,000 sq ft of retail shopping space and this standard is generally accepted in out-of-town developments in North America[7]. Parking provision in Great Britain is generally well below this level at present.

The replies of respondents to our questionnaire on the future pattern of retailing suggested that by 1980 the standards required will only approximate to those which are current on the Continent in 1970, and we consider that the median figures (of 5.75 parking places per 1,000 sq ft of shopping space in central shopping areas, of 5.0 in suburban centres, and 8.5 in out-of-town centres), if used, should be regarded as the bare minimum and that every effort should be made to improve on them.

Shortage of space in this country makes it inevitable that virtually all major car park construction in city centres, and much elsewhere, will be multi-storey. Even in North American out-of-town centres where the space consideration is not paramount to the same degree, the distance from vehicle to shop is becoming so great that multi-storey parking is being contemplated[7].

The expenditure involved in multi-storey car park construction, apart from any other considerations, makes it inevitable that the shopper will have to pay to park near shopping centres. Neither of the consumer surveys showed any sign that shoppers objected to paying for parking as such (although there were a few comments from people who thought they had to pay too much). What they were more concerned with was the convenience of the car parks they used: in this regard it is relevant to note that 'convenience' is different for a supermarket shopper (who may have a heavy load to carry) than for the customer of a department store (whose load may be relatively light).

From this point of view the RICA survey showed that multi-storey parks are less favoured than ground level parks: many respondents said they would be prepared to walk farther – and some even to pay more – for ground level parking if the choice existed.

The major objections seem to be that lifts are frequently small, few and extremely slow, stairs are steep, and pram ramps are usually absent. These are points of basic design which might well receive a good deal more attention, and this is more likely to be the case where a multi-storey park is of integrated design with the shopping centre, as at Chester, Wolverhampton and Doncaster (Arndale) than where it is a separate entity.

Public transport Public transport here means the bus rather than the train: the Office's pavement surveys revealed only a minute proportion of shoppers who had come in by train (only 4 out of 479). This does not mean that a suitably placed underground station would not make an impact: there are many instances both in Europe and North America where subway stations have been integrated into major new shopping developments. But there is virtually no such experience to draw on in this country.

Over a third of the shoppers interviewed in the pavement survey conducted by EDC staff had come in by bus. This indicates a level of bus use much greater than in the USA where public transport has declined much more[2].

The amount that people use buses as opposed to cars varies between different parts of the country, there being some correlation between car ownership in a given area and the proportion of shoppers using cars. If such a correlation is maintained over the next few years, during which time the number of private cars will double, and by the end of which the great majority of households will have the use of a car, the inferences for both parking provision and public transport are apparent.

All the surveys of retailers' opinion served to stress the importance attached by retailers to bus transport.

Buses may serve a centre in two ways. Local buses may pass the centre, or it may be adjacent to a terminus for country buses. Ideally, local buses should pass by immediately outside a precinct: the IMR survey suggested that they are unlikely to be effective if they are more than five minutes walk away.

The proximity of a country bus station was not considered to be nearly as important, but some of the most successful centres studied have a country bus station very close by, or even integrated into the design: examples of this are Norwich (St Stephens St) and Doncaster (Arndale). The performance of the Waterdale precinct at Doncaster was at first deleteriously affected by the fact that the bus station nearby was so designed that passengers tended to approach the main centre of the town by a route which by-passed the precinct.

Generous provision of bus services does not in itself guarantee success: as indicated above, the Seacroft centre at Leeds has been a marked failure despite such provision.

The importance of bus services to shopping centres in future years may depend very much on whether such services are promoted or whether they are allowed to decline – ie whether the UK follows European practice as at, for example, CAP 3000 at Nice, Skahölmen near Stockholm and the Nordwestzenstrum, Frankfurt, or whether it follows American practice: this question is examined in more depth in Chapter 7. Our evidence suggests a 'European' approach may prevail: towns like Nottingham, Doncaster, Preston and Norwich evidently envisaged a continued rôle for the bus in the way that bus stations are being sited in relation to shopping developments. On the other hand Cumbernauld has been criticised by residents because they feel that the town is too orientated towards cars and there is insufficient provision for public transport[9].

A factor which may well be of importance is the design of buses. Generally speaking, buses as constructed at present are not well designed for those with a heavy load of purchases.

Integration with existing pedestrian routes

Easy pedestrian access and integration with existing pedestrian routes were considered matters of prime importance in the surveys undertaken among retailers.

Multiple shops considered that the most successful developments were those which were complementary to established locations and which reinforced current shopping habits. Therefore the development must be sited on (but not necessarily along) existing shopping thoroughfares and should encourage pedestrian flow.

What all this sums up to is that shoppers should be able to find and see a new development in the course of their normal shopping route and that they should have some incentive to enter and pass through it. Examples of failure to understand and apply these principles were found in a number of developments which have not been successful, for example the Waterdale development at Doncaster, the Main centre at Derby, the Tricorn development at Portsmouth and the Elephant and Castle shopping centre. Each of these developments is worth examining in more detail, as they all illustrate different aspects of this general point.

The Waterdale centre at Doncaster erred in two important respects. It is by no means easy to find if one is in the central area of Doncaster (a number of people interviewed in the Arndale Centre had either not heard of it or did not know where to find it). The original plans for this development envisaged a direct pedestrian approach to one of the main central streets, but this was never provided. Also, the adjacent bus station was built so that pedestrians preferred to leave it and go directly to the centre of Doncaster, by-passing the Waterdale precinct (and they still prefer to do so despite the fact that access to the Waterdale centre has been much improved and pedestrians have to clamber over barriers and cross a busy main road in order to take their former route). This suggests that it is much easier and more desirable to make use of an existing pedestrian flow than to try to divert it.

The Main centre at Derby is also hard to find if one is at the central part of Derby: in fact the entrance is sited at a point where few shops are found, and well away from the major shops (in fairness it should be stated that the pedestrian flows in the town will inevitably change when the inner ring road and associated car parks are completed and the new corporation shopping centre is built: in fact the developers seem to be banking on this). Besides being too far from the town centre, this development was insufficiently strong to stand by itself.

The Tricorn centre at Portsmouth is not directly accessible from the main street. This may not matter so much since several major shops fronting on the main street have back entrances giving on to the centre, and there is a thriving fruit and vegetable market in Charlotte Street. In fact in 1969, the few shops open which faced on Charlotte Street, were busy. But there was nothing to draw anybody through the development. The pedestrians who did penetrate to the farther side were faced with an inner ring road with traffic moving at great speed, with a few acres of derelict land on the other side. Again, it is fair to say that future development plans may change this.

There is unimpeded access to the Elephant and Castle shopping area only from one direction, the Walworth Road, and even here there is a break in shopping caused by the railway. But even if a shopper does penetrate to the outside of the shopping centre she is confronted by a complex system of ramps involving a circuitous approach to the doors; so far from making it easy for her to enter, she must wonder if an effort is not being made to keep her out.

On the other hand, the Grosvenor-Laing centre at Chester and the St George's centre at Preston are examples of centres where pedestrian movement was carefully studied at the inception of the scheme. At Chester the malls have been integrated with an existing Victorian arcade (St Michael's Row) with great success. At Preston great care was taken to study the movements of shoppers emerging

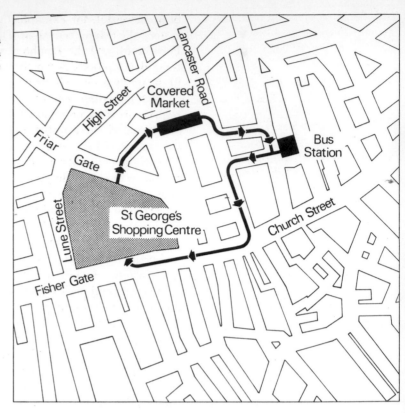

Figure 5
The pedestrian route through Preston, showing the location of the St George's Centre

from the bus station, and it was found that there was a traditional shopping route which varied surprisingly little (see Figure 5). The St George's Centre was sited to take account of this, and it was estimated (correctly) that its position on the traditional shopping route would go a long way to ensure success. It would appear that this kind of detailed study of what people actually do (as opposed to making assumptions about what they should or might do) is essential, yet it is not always undertaken.

Visibility of the centre from a main thoroughfare

Our research suggested that visibility of the centre and of all the shops in it from a main thoroughfare was a factor of great importance.

To some extent this is tied in with integration with existing shopping routes (see above): if a precinct is sited outside the normal circulation pattern few people will see it because few get that far anyway. But a number of the centres studied appeared to have done less well than they might have done because only a fraction of the shops were visible from the main access point, for example, the Duckworth Square precinct, and the Main Centre at Derby, and the Seacroft centre at Leeds.

The single mall type of layout, to which American practice is tending[7] offers the great advantage that all the shops are immediately visible from the entrance to the precinct.

Absence of traffic

Attitudes here, as shown by the surveys, appear to be conflicting. It seems that the absence of traffic is appreciated by consumers more than by retailers, and that it is not taken into account by firms as a positive factor before going into a precinct.

The main reason for this apparent lack of interest on the part of retailers is probably that they take it for granted. It is very unlikely that any new major development in this country will not be free from traffic, not only for reasons of safety, but also to provide a 'civilised environment' for shopping. The question then becomes one of the degree to which traffic can be excluded from existing shopping streets, as in many continental centres such as Essen.

An extremely successful project was undertaken in Norwich to close London Street: this was finally done in July 1967 and proved wrong the fears of those traders who opposed it. Since the closure, trade in London Street has advanced considerably, some shops reporting turnover increases of 25 per cent, and the street has been widely acclaimed as a model for future developments of this type. The street has now been completely paved over and provided with trees, shrub boxes, seats and an outdoor cafe[10] (see photograph).

A pedestrianisation scheme was introduced to a rather larger area in Bolton in 1969. Evidence on trading performance is hard to assess, since only 40 per cent of the traders answered queries on this point, but a concurrent survey of shoppers showed that 76 per cent were in favour of the change[11].

The UK has nothing to be ashamed of in its record of building new traffic-free centres: Coventry led the world when it was built, and the new towns, if they were not traffic-free from the beginning, are virtually all free from traffic now. But our record of removing traffic from existing shopping streets is poor: the many European towns and cities which have achieved foot streets are matched by a mere handful in this country, of which Norwich, Bradford and Bolton with their so far limited essays, are the outstanding examples, though a number of other towns have planned schemes for the future. Particular attention needs to be paid to facilities for the receipt and despatch of goods, to car parking and to access by public transport, but we would urge that a far more determined effort should be made in the coming years to achieve that separation of pedestrians and vehicular traffic which is already becoming commonplace in continental cities. The limited experience in this country suggests that many objections may vanish during the relatively short initial experimental period of closure.

Weather protection

Weather protection emerged as a factor to which great importance was attached in almost all the retailer attitude surveys, and was among the favourable factors quoted in the pavement surveys of shoppers.

In the British climate the degree of importance attached to covered walkways is not surprising, and virtually all major new centres are provided at least with some form of canopy. Even so, the view of multiple shops was that protection from rain does not itself draw people to a centre; rather, it benefits trade by persuading people to remain in the centre when the weather becomes bad.

A basic requirement which multiple shops regarded as critical was avoidance of wind. They stated that main streets should not be aligned with prevailing winds and the presence of tall structures should not create air turbulence. Several centres have been gravely affected by the latter: the St George's centre, Croydon and the Merrion centre, Leeds, had to be roofed over because of the gales created by high buildings, and one of the most frequent causes of complaint found in the pavement survey of Cowley concerned the draughts created by a tower block of flats in the middle of the precinct.

That at least covered walkways should be provided is not in dispute. What is a more debatable point is whether centres should be fully covered and enclosed or not.

The surveys of retailers would suggest that there is little demand for them. The results of our pavement surveys of shoppers, however, suggest the opposite conclusion.

Considering the order of 'success' or 'attraction' by the ratio of favourable to unfavourable comments, the three most successful centres – Crossgates, Chester and Doncaster (Arndale) – were all covered centres.

Covered centres scored on warmth, atmosphere and weather protection, and open centres received many adverse comments regarding lack of adequate weather protection.

An explanation of respondents' attitudes was found when respondents were asked whether they would prefer to shop in (a) a fully covered centre; (b) a partly covered centre; or (c) a centre with canopies over the front of the shops. In towns containing covered centres (Chester, Doncaster and Leeds) 187 out of 211 respondents, or 89 per cent favoured covered centres. In towns containing only open centres 132 out of 268, or 49 per cent opted for covered centres. An identical question was asked in the RICA survey: here, in Norwich and Stevenage only 12 per cent and 19 per cent opted for covered centres. Neither of these towns contains a covered centre, and one is led to the conclusion that respondents' attitudes depend almost wholly on knowledge: there was resistance to the idea of covered centres in places where shoppers had no experience of them, whereas in places where they were familiar they were favoured. (There is a further reason for the divergence of the RICA figures: their interviews were conducted at respondents' homes in the hottest summer for years; the pavement surveys were conducted out of doors in a rather inclement winter.)

Further evidence comes from the Office questionnaire on the future pattern of retailing. Respondents were asked what they thought the reaction of retailers, consumers and developers would be to shopping centres with covered malls. The general expectation was that consumers and developers would view such developments with favour, and that even retailers would be at least neutral. (See Appendix C.)

The conclusion of the sub-committee is therefore that multiple shop respondents are wrong in thinking, as interviews at head offices suggested they thought, that totally enclosed centres in this country are premature. The sub-committee's evidence suggests that shoppers regard them favourably, and the covered centres examined in the survey were all commercially successful. Furthermore, active consideration was being given by the developers to roofing over at least two of the open centres which were visited.

The team from the Capital and Counties Property Company which visited North America to study shopping centre developments found that:

'The implications of enclosure do not stop with building the roof and air conditioning the mall. The centre really becomes one large building and a single trading unit, more akin to leasing space in an enormous department store and for this reason, as the Americans now appreciate, it is important that detailing, finishes and shop fronts are designed to provide a unified whole'[7].

While some progress has been made with building covered centres in this country, it does not seem that as yet all the implications of such construction have been realised. Two factors especially need to be considered: the relation of the individual shops to the mall, with particular reference to the nature of the shop front, and the desirable level of lighting.

In the earlier covered centres, both in the USA and in this country, shops within the centre looked very much the same from the outside as shops in an ordinary high street. The Bull Ring is an example of this: most of the shop fronts could easily be found outside, and one shopfitter even fitted rain dripboards. The shopper enters the unit as she would an ordinary shop.

But this rather loses much of the advantage of a covered shopping centre: the shopper should not have to enter the shop since in a sense she is in it already. Slide up or slide away shop fronts are now readily accepted by tenants in North America and Europe, but they are far from being general here, even in the more advanced centres.

In order to present a harmonious and attractive appearance it is generally agreed that rigid control should be exerted over the design of individual shop fascias, even if only their height above floor level. Some developers go further: they may dictate the form of the fascia altogether, leaving the title to the tenant (as at Runcorn).

With regard to lighting, it is considered in North America that by reducing the standard of daylight a lower level of artificial lighting in the mall results in a greater visual concentration on the shop fronts[7]. In most of the centres studied mall lighting was fairly low, contrasting with brilliant shop window illumination. Continental practice appears to be similar.

The approach in some British developments appears to be rather different: the level of lighting at the Bull Ring has been raised considerably since it was first opened, and Grosvenor Estates, after their experience of the Chester Development, are providing a much higher level of illumination at the new Runcorn centre. It may well be that the British do not like entering gloomy buildings: after all, in our climate it is usually gloomy enough outside. Nevertheless, there seem strong grounds for thinking that American practice will be followed in many instances.

Number of levels Many Multiple Shops Federation respondents interviewed were opposed to the idea of multi-level centres.

Obviously there can be disadvantages, and it is not difficult to find developments where units on the top storey remained unoccupied for long periods (eg the Elephant and Castle, the Armdale Centre at Doncaster, the Callender development at Falkirk). Even when both floors are occupied, it may well be that there is a considerable rent differential between the lower and upper floors (as at the Whitgift centre, Croydon; at the St George's Centre, Preston, however, the rents are equal on the two floors).

But our surveys of pedestrians did not suggest that multi-level centres in themselves deterred shoppers. Two of the most popular centres were multi-level, and when respondents were asked if they would be troubled by having to shop in a multi-level centre 85 per cent said 'no' and only 15 per cent said 'yes'.

Furthermore, in our questionnaire on the future pattern of retailing respondents were asked whether the various main types of shopping developments erected from 1975 onwards would be single or multi-storey. The vote was decisively for multi-storey developments in city centres and single-storey developments elsewhere.

There were however reservations, and these were brought out by many respondents in the pavement surveys. These mainly concern access, which must be:

1 Available at all points. The Preston St George's centre was particularly criticised because, although it has adequate access at the end, there is none in the middle.

2 Appropriate for all classes of shoppers. This is a matter of some

difficulty: the old and infirm dislike escalators and may find stairs awkward; mothers with prams require pram ramps; few have a good word to say for the lifts usually provided, which are small, slow and insufficient in numbers.

The most successful solutions to the problem involve the provision of stairs, escalators and pram ramps. A moving ramp will cater for almost everyone but is expensive and requires an extravagant amount of space if a suitably low gradient is to be achieved; nevertheless it has been adopted in a few cases where the scale of the centre is large enough to take one (Whitgift, Croydon; Greyfriars, Ipswich; and Merrion, Leeds). In some recent European developments the angle of slope of moving ramps has been made much steeper than that usual in this country. These ramps have proved successful, and they may be adopted with success here.

Not only should access within the centre be adequate, but access from outside should enable both floors to be approached naturally from the outside. St George's Centre, Preston is a particularly happy answer to this problem: the lower level is entered directly from Lune Street and the upper level directly from Fishergate Street, while in Friargate Street both levels are approached by sloping pavements with a very low gradient. This is, of course, possible because the centre is built on a sloping site. However, in the majority of cases natural access on a level from outside cannot be provided to both storeys.

If people cannot be led into the upper level naturally, then the same effect can be achieved by design. This is in many cases achieved by building car parks above, or on a level with, the top floor (eg the Arndale centre at Doncaster, the Wulfrun and Mander centres at Wolverhampton). People emerging from the car park are channelled into the top level.

It is important to have magnets on all floors of a multi-level precinct if both levels are to succeed: the Arndale developments at Doncaster and Stretford provide good examples of this: these should be compared with the effects of the failure to attract magnets to the top floors of the Elephant and Castle development.

The key argument in favour of multi-storey centres arises when they are considered together with covered centres: the latter are more economic to construct if they are built on more than one level.

High land costs, if nothing else, are likely to force the provision of multi-level centres in town centres, and the evidence we have been able to gather suggests that consumers are prepared to accept them provided the basic principles of 'pedestrian engineering' are understood and applied. Early centres provided several examples of failure where these principles were not understood, but examination of centres recently and currently being built suggests that developers are learning them fast. We would anticipate that there will be far greater numbers of multi-level covered centres built in coming years. North American and European experience suggests that the increased expenditure is more than compensated by increased returns.

Pedestrian flow within the centre

A factor of importance is the simplicity or complexity of the routes the pedestrian has to follow. Early American centres had complicated circulation arrangements, with clusters of units standing like islands in the middle of a sea of pedestrians. Later practice has tended to a straight line flow as the ideal, with occasional variations (an 'L' or 'T' shape, or a dumbbell)[7]. Practice in both Britain and Europe has tended to follow this line.

This point is illustrated in Figure 6. The oldest centre is an example of a complicated circulation arrangement. The two later centres approximate much more closely to a straight line flow.

A factor constantly being cited as an attractive factor by respondents in our pavement surveys of shoppers was compactness: this was mentioned by over a fifth of all respondents, and suggests that the precinct idea is inherently more attractive to shoppers than the usual extended High Street. Compactness really means minimising the amount of walking required to go round all the shops. This may be achieved by reducing the intrusion of access for goods either by providing such access at first floor level (as at Keighley and Duckworth Square) or in a basement (as at Princess Hay, Exeter) or peripherally – as is normal in Europe and North America whenever land availability permits.

We have already discussed above some of the principles of pedestrian engineering: the siting of access from car parks and the disposition of 'magnets'. Another important factor is the width of the shopping mall in a pedestrian development. There are two main considerations here, which hitherto have been held to conflict. From the point of view of encouraging impulse shopping the mall should be narrow: possibly 25 feet would be most effective. From the point of view of amenity the mall should be wide – 80 feet has been suggested. In many cases a compromise width of 40 to 50 feet has been adopted in both Britain and America, but there is some evidence that in both countries malls are being built rather narrower in order to encourage shoppers to cross from one side to the other.

Good individual shop design

Indications were that this is important, particularly the provision of adequate storage space and adequate access. We have not been able to do enough work on this to make meaningful comments beyond pointing out the importance of these factors: they need to be quantified in a way which was beyond the limits of what our research could do. However, the Multiple Shops Federation[12] has made useful recommendations regarding service access.

A factor which is connected with shop design is flexibility. Respondents to the questionnaire on the future pattern of retailing were asked if they thought provision should be made for shops of different sizes in new developments:

1 By modular construction which would permit flexibility of division

2 By forecasting what number of shops would be of different shapes and sizes and building accordingly

3 By consultation with prospective lessees.

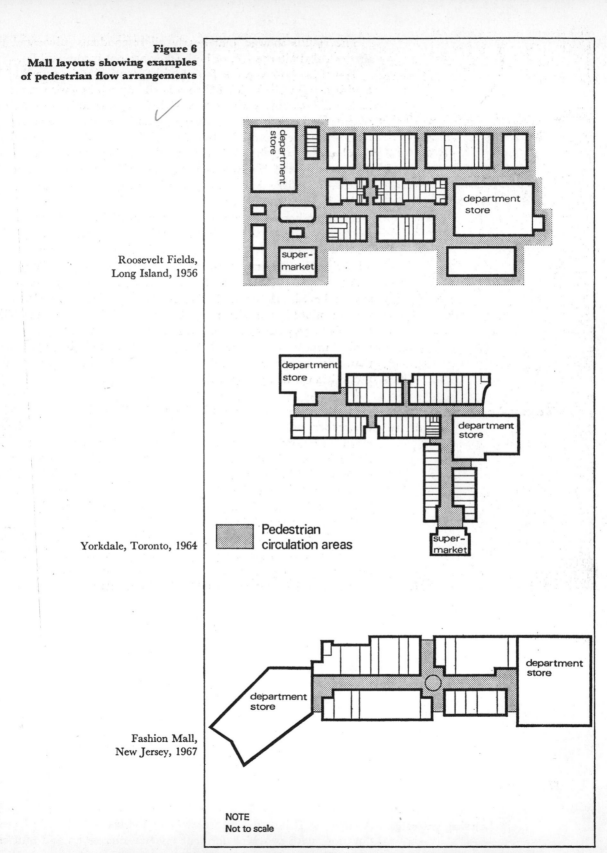

Figure 6
Mall layouts showing examples
of pedestrian flow arrangements

Roosevelt Fields,
Long Island, 1956

department
store

department
store

super-
market

Yorkdale, Toronto, 1964

department
store

department
store

super-
market

Pedestrian
circulation areas

Fashion Mall,
New Jersey, 1967

department
store

department
store

NOTE
Not to scale

Plans by courtesy of Capital and Counties Property Company Limited

The results showed that nearly all respondents advocated the first or third alternative, or both (they are not incompatible).

Too often, however, one finds rows of identical units separated by load-bearing walls which offer no flexibility whatsoever except the rather unsatisfactory strategems of dividing one unit between two tenants, or having a larger shop substantially divided by a row of load-bearing columns. Waterdale and Duckworth Square – both developments which failed to attract their full quota of tenants – are good examples of this, but even at St George's, Preston – a successful centre – dissatisfaction was expressed with the lack of flexibility of design by a number of tenants.

On the other hand some of the more up-to-date centres have full flexibility, using curtain walls as partitions rather than load-bearing party walls: examples of this are the Bull Ring and the Runcorn and Victoria (Nottingham) centres currently under construction.

A point that is relevant here is the degree of permanence which should be aimed for in building shopping developments. With present materials a shopping development's physical durability extends to 50 years or more. But retailing methods are changing so rapidly that in future years it may be desirable to build for no more than 20 years at most. The degree to which this will be a practicable proposition will depend on the materials available.

Tenants' associations and publicity

Of the centres studied most had a traders' association of one kind or another, but they were of greatly varying degrees of strength and effectiveness, being strongest at the covered Arndale centres, at the Bull Ring and in the Grosvenor Laing precinct at Chester. Elsewhere the initiative has largely been left to shopkeepers with all too often the results found at Seacroft, which suffered from the lack of interest of the multiples and large firms, with a consequent limitation of the amount of publicity which could be organised[3].

Standards of promotion varied in the centres studied. At the covered developments seen frequent displays were held within the developments, together with events like carol concerts and mannequin shows. In most of the other developments promotion was left very much to the traders themselves.

Generally speaking, it was only in the centres with a strong tenants' association with which the landlord worked in full co-operation that any really imaginative attempt at promotion was made. In the absence of this close bond there is no incentive to promotional activities. It has been suggested that in the case of a successful scheme neither landlord nor tenant feels the need for joint promotions, whereas in an unsuccessful one tenants will feel unenthusiastic about what they feel to be subsidising their landlord's publicity for an inferior scheme[13]. There is obviously sound sense in such an attitude and it can only be overcome by the kind of landlord-tenant co-operation commonplace in the larger American centres[7] [14].

Leasing practice

A common British practice now is for the leases to be of 21 years duration, with provision for rent reviews after seven and fourteen years. There appears, however, to be a tendency for leases in shopping centres to be getting shorter (originally 49 or 99 years was not uncommon): one major developer is shortly to introduce 15 year leases with reviews every five years[2].

This means that there is risk of an inflexibility which can face a developer with an awkward choice between lowering rents or losing his tenants if trade is bad. An example of this inflexibility can be seen in a comparison between the Crossgates Centre at Leeds where concessionary rents were offered in the first three years, and the Seacroft centre, where the rental was in the first instance the usual type described above. Concessions were offered too late, and in too haphazard a manner, to save the centre[3].

Turnover based rentals, usual in North America[7] [14], are not common at present, though instances are found (eg at the Bull Ring and at the Victoria Centre, Nottingham currently under construction). The main reason has been the objection on the part of retailers to giving in effect a proportion of the equity to the developer but other obstacles are the attitude of financial institutions and (probably most intractable) the difficulty that such rentals might raise in the operation of the Landlord and Tenant Act.

While the rental structure may not be of prime importance in a really successful centre, and is immaterial in a really unsuccessful one, it might be critical in a borderline one. Prospective tenants, particularly small independents, would have far more incentive to take risks in a scheme offering carefully calculated concessionary rentals than in a scheme where they had no idea at the outset whether poor business was likely to be transient or permanent and they did not know if they were going to be able to take enough to cover their rent.

Amenities The sub-committee considers the provision of a high standard of amenities of great importance. While such things as play areas, seats, public lavatories and an aesthetic ambiance did not emerge as major factors affecting the *commercial* success of a centre, the research carried out by RICA underlined their importance to shoppers in creating a comfortable place for them to shop in. Such comfort may well not bring a direct and apparent financial return, but more market research among consumers on these points and consultation with such bodies as consumer groups could go a long way towards ensuring that shopping centres become more pleasant places to shop in.

One point which is of considerable importance in connection with amenities is the provision made for the disabled. For example, all too often one finds that the design of a shopping centre incorporates features like short flights of steps which present no problem to the able, but which are a major obstacle to anyone unfortunate enough to depend on a wheelchair.

The Chronically Sick and Disabled Persons Act, 1970 (among other things) places an obligation on anyone converting or erecting buildings, to which the public are admitted, to make provisions for the needs of disabled people in so far as it is both reasonable and practical in the circumstance. This provision relates specifically to access both into and within the building, access to parking facilities and to toilets. The accompanying Ministry circular (DHSS 12/70) specifically states that the above applies to shops.

The sub-committee hopes that local authorities, architects and developers concerned with shops and shopping centres will ensure that these provisions are implemented liberally in favour of the disabled.

Another aspect of this is the provision of what may broadly be called leisure facilities. At least one New Town centre has been criticised on the grounds that it is dead and lifeless once the shops shut[5] and it may be suspected that similar criticisms could be made both of other new towns and of major developments in existing towns. Although the sub-committee's research did not suggest that leisure facilities were a factor of commercial importance, it may well be questioned whether a major development that dies at six in the evening is playing its part as a town centre or a considerable part of one. Continental practice seems to tend toward the provision of leisure facilities like cinemas and restaurants in shopping centres. In North America shopping centres seem to concentrate more on trade – possibly because of the much greater mobility and dispersion of the population.

The growing problem of vandalism is, however, relevant here. It has often been said that shopping centres should be a pleasure to walk through at night as well as day, but this is hardly likely to be possible if they become the haunt of undesirable elements like tramps, 'junkies' and hooligans. Security guards, though effective in many instances, are sometimes faced with situations which might more properly be handled by the police. Discussion with local authorities, developers and shopkeepers suggests that there may be a tendency to provide gates to precincts which can be closed when the shops are shut. This might be a pity in many ways but the bodies concerned can hardly be blamed if they act in this manner.

References

1 Models Working Group, *Urban Models in Shopping Studies*, NEDO, 1970
2 C. S. Jones, *Regional Shopping Centres*, Business Books, 1969
3 D Roper, unpublished thesis, Liverpool University
4 Department of Town and Country Planning, University of Manchester, *Regional Shopping Centres in North West England*, 1964
5 C H Byron, *Basildon: Shopping, Work for Women, Leisure*, Basildon Development Corporation 1967
6 Multiple Shops Federation, *The Planning of Shopping Centres*, 1964
7 Capital and Counties Property Co Ltd, *Shopping for Pleasure*, 1969
8 V Gruen and L Smith, *Shopping Towns USA*
9 A J M Sykes, J M Livingstone and M Green, *Cumbernauld: a Household Survey and Report*, Occupational paper No 1, University of Strathclyde Department of Sociology, 1967
10 A A Wood 'Shopping centres and their form', paper given to BIM conference *Problems in Shop and Store Location*, April 1970
11 R H Ogden 'Pedestrian precinct in Bolton' *Journal of the Town Planning Institute*, Vol 56, No 4, April 1970
12 Multiple Shops Federation, *Standards for Service Areas in Shopping Centres*, 1968
13 E Rutherford Young, 'Promotions', *Shop Property*, Vol 2, No 2, March/April 1969
14 Capital and Counties Property Co Ltd, *Design for Shopping* 1970

Chapter 6 Where people will shop

There are several different kinds of shopping area, and the replies to our questionnaire on the future pattern of shopping, together with analysis of existing trends, suggests that the share of total turnover accounted for by some types is likely to change significantly by 1980.

They may be listed as follows:

1   Areas unlikely to change their share of trade much
(a)   Central shopping areas
(b)   Shops in villages and small towns

2   Areas likely to increase their share of trade
(a)   Suburban shopping centres

3   Areas likely to lose trade
(a)   Street corner shops
(b)   Shops in intermediate areas adjacent to town centres
(c)   'Parades' of the type built in the 1930s

4   Areas whose performance will depend on the attitude of public authorities
(a)   'Off-centre' stores
(b)   Free-standing superstores
(c)   Out-of-town regional shopping centres.

Central shopping areas*   Such centres in major towns offer a full range to the shopper, from 'convenience' shops through 'durable' shops to shops of a high degree of specialisation in some of the most important centres.

As the standard of living has risen over the decades, more and more people have been able to visit central shopping areas of major towns, and the weekly shopping trip is an accepted feature of many families' lives. Between the wars, such trips were mostly made by public transport, and even now, particularly in the North of England, the structure of bus routes remains and is still used.

But more and more people now use their cars as their chief means of transport for all purposes, including shopping. The effects of this process are well known and were cogently discussed in the Buchanan Report[1]. We do not need to reiterate the way cars have caused congestion and pollution in town centres, but it is within the broad terms of our brief to consider what effect all this is going to have on the pattern of shopping, and particularly on shopping in central shopping areas.

In 1968 there were 0.2 cars per head of population in Great Britain[2], or 10.6 million cars. By 1980, the Road Research Laboratory calculates, there will be about 20 million cars†. An answer given to a question in our questionnaire on the future pattern of retailing

---

* See Glossary
† The figures given are 19.4 million, or 20.6 million, according to the saturation level assumed. The difference, which becomes more marked as the projection advances past the year 2000, is not critical to this argument

suggested that 25 per cent of all shopping journeys would be made by car as opposed to 10 to 12 per cent in 1968. This may be a low estimate.

The implications for the future of shopping in major town centres are profound. Many – perhaps most – town centres are barely coping with the increase in use of the motor car that has taken place up till now. And the degree to which town centre shopping remains an attractive proposition will depend almost wholly on central and local government's success in dealing with this problem.

Broadly speaking, it might possibly be tackled in four ways:

1   By the provision of adequate public transport and the incentive to use it

2   By building adequate car parks and access roads

3   By excluding cars from the centre altogether (ie pedestrianisation)

4   By restricting the development of a town centre and concentrating on the provision of other types of shopping (eg in suburban centres).

These approaches are not mutually exclusive and in particular (2) and (3) may form complementary approaches in a given situation.

Public transport   The history of public transport since the war has been mainly one of erosion, partly because of spiralling costs, mainly because the private car is a more convenient and flexible means of travelling.

The problems involved in the competition between public transport and the car do not affect this country alone, although the effective action of public authorities varies in different countries. In the USA the erosion of public transport is far greater[3]; in Europe some authorities appear to have been rather more successful in preventing decay striking the public transport system, especially by extending the underground passenger network[4] [5] [6]. In some British towns, such as Coventry, there has been an imaginative attempt to induce the shopper to travel by public transport, and at the proposed new town of Milton Keynes careful consideration has been given to the establishment of a viable public transport system[7].

The sub-committee feels that an effective public transport system is of great importance for shopping, and urges that this should receive more attention from transport planners than in the past. At the same time, it must be recognised that the experience of European town planners who have consciously tried to maintain the position of town centres by manipulating traffic and encouraging the use of public transport has forced them to acknowledge that, taken by itself, this sort of policy is insufficient[8].

Adequate car parks and access roads   Whether the provision of these is possible is largely a question of the cost, the configuration of the town and the economic usefulness of existing buildings. In many towns (eg Oxford and Chester) the extent to which car parks can be provided is limited, and even where the buildings are of commercial as opposed to historic interest there are obviously limits to the number of car parks that can be built.

If car parks cannot be built within the shopping area they may be built outside it. Here one must consider how far the shopper is willing to walk with her purchases. It has been said that she wants the car boot as close to the check-out as possible when she makes her main weekly trip for groceries and certainly few car shoppers will face with equanimity the prospect of staggering half a mile with anything up to a hundredweight of food.

The question then arises of what parking standards* local authorities should adopt for shopping developments.

In 1967 the Road Research Laboratory conducted a survey[9] among 83 county borough authorities (of whom 73 replied) asking inter alia:

1 If the authority had adopted any parking standard
2 If so, what was the standard for shops
3 Whether it was found practicable to adhere to them.

The results may be summarised as in Table 4.

Table 4   Distribution of parking standards, 1966

Standard measured in car spaces per 1,000 sq ft floorspace (gross)	Standard adhered to	Standard not adhered to	Standard given only as a guide	Recently adopted	Total
5	1	—	1	—	2
4	2	—	—	—	2
3–3.9	—	—	—	1	1
2–2.9	3	8	4	1	16
1–1.9	7	4	—	1	12
Less than 1	1	4	2	1	8
Variable standard	4	5	1	—	10
Other form of standard	—	—	2	—	2
Values not available	—	—	—	—	1
No standard	—	—	—	—	19
Total	18	21	10	4	73

Thus it appeared not only that the standards adopted were modest (although it is commented that they would depend on the price of land, the provision of other parking in the town and various other factors), but that in the majority of cases they could not be enforced.

The limitation of horizons is further shown by an answer to our questionnaire of the future pattern of retailing. We asked what the standard of car park spaces per thousand sq ft of shopping space should be for central shopping areas by 1975 and 1980, and the median answers were three and six respectively (see Appendix C).

Very few estimates were for as much as ten spaces per 1000 sq ft, but this is the figure at which Continental and American centres are now developing.

* See Glossary

Pedestrianisation

Most of the centres built in New Towns are for pedestrians only (eg Stevenage, Basildon from the start; others like Bracknell and Crawley have been restructured to become so). Of course in these cases pedestrianisation provides little difficulty, since when building on a 'green field' site the necessary access routes etc can be planned right from the beginning. Again, the building of a pedestrian centre at Coventry, flattened during the war, presented an imaginative answer to the challenge of reconstruction.

The problems really arise in the case of old towns, where the physical difficulties may be considerable. Despite this, plans for pedestrianisation in whole or in part are going ahead in a number of towns (eg Norwich, Bolton, Weymouth, Portsmouth and Derby).

We have already considered the question of pedestrianisation in Chapter 5; it is sufficient to say that the principle that new central precincts should be traffic-free is by now generally accepted, but that comparatively few efforts to exclude traffic from existing precincts have been made. The sub-committee's opinion is that the opposition sometimes met when such schemes are proposed is short-sighted; experience both in Europe and in the limited essays in the UK has shown that provided adequate provision is made for parking, public transport and the access of goods, such schemes are unlikely to involve losses to traders and provide a much more civilised environment for shopping.

Diversion of trade to other types of centre

We have already considered some of the difficulties involved in the traditional concentration of uses in the town centre. But it may well be possible to disperse some of them to other locations. This should not be detrimental to the town centre but rather provide the elbow-room which would enable uses essentially located in the central area to develop and maintain the dominance of the town centre. Even though shopping is a traditional and very valuable central area use it should be examined in this way.

We discuss the potentialities of the various kinds of shopping centres to which town centre trade might be diverted (suburban centres and the different kinds of out-of-town centre).

The point which needs emphasis is that if, in a given town, measures taken with regard to public transport, access and parking and pedestrianisation are insufficient to produce an uncongested, civilised environment, shoppers will take their custom elsewhere anyway. A local authority may well be faced, therefore, with a choice between a *planned* diversion of trade and an *unplanned* diminution of trade with consequent damage to the quality of commerce and of life generally in the centre. In some cases making the right choice may involve a more 'interventionist' attitude on the part of government at a higher level, since a local authority will naturally be reluctant to see trade diverted outside its own boundaries. (We examine the effect of circumscribed local authority boundaries in Chapter 7.)

Shops in villages and small towns

This is hardly a homogeneous group, and the factors that are most critical here are likely to vary from one place to another.

The critical factors appear to be:

1 *Increased use of the car*. This will mean that the inhabitants of villages and small towns will find major centres increasingly accessible.

2 *The drift from the land*. Opportunities for younger people are frequently slight in the country and the tendency for them to seek their livelihood in towns will probably continue[10].

3 *Retirement*. People are living longer and retiring earlier: certainly in the more clement areas of the country increasing numbers are leaving the larger towns to spend their retirement in smaller towns and in the country.

4 *Second homes*. It seems likely also that increasing personal incomes will enable a significant number of people to acquire second homes – weekend cottages or holiday houses – outside the major towns.

These factors are very difficult to quantify. The first two of them will tend to decrease spending in villages and small towns, the latter two to increase it. In terms of overall expenditure these tendencies may cancel each other out. But it seems likely that there will be a shift in the pattern of expenditure. People will visit major centres by car to buy comparison goods – it is hardly worth travelling fifty miles to buy the same groceries as exist in the local store – and the exodus of young people will mean the loss of people who are about to set up home – another loss of durable expenditure. These losses are unlikely to be made up by the surplus of elderly folk or weekenders: the former spend comparatively little on durables, the latter do their spending mostly in their primary place of residence. So outside the major towns there is likely to be an even greater emphasis on convenience as opposed to durable goods. This may entail an appreciable reduction in the total number of shops, and supermarkets may be able to account for an increasing proportion of expenditure in these areas.

Suburban shopping centres   We have already pointed out the possibility of diverting some central area trade to suburban centres in order to lessen the strain on town centres. In some places – Birmingham, for instance – there has always been a strong tradition of suburban shopping. In others, such as Sunderland, no such tradition exists, and developers have found difficulty in attracting trade to a suburban centre in a town orientated towards central area shopping.

As has been pointed out above, the respondents to our questionnaire on the future pattern of retailing foresaw that by 1980 the proportion of total trade carried on in suburban shopping centres would increase by over a quarter. This implies a considerable diversion of trade over the country as a whole, largely from locations other than central areas, and also implies the dedication of a large amount of capital to the construction of such centres.

To some extent this process is happening naturally as part of the changing morphology of towns. Part of the research we carried out – and we shall return to this later – was an examination of the way in which shopping outside the central shopping area was changing. Preston, for example, was a town where the shopping pattern was originally rather like the spokes of a wheel, with the main shopping centre at the hub. Through time the inner end of the radial streets started to decay – a process which was hastened by reconstruction in the town centre and the building of an inner ring road. But the shops at outer extremes of the radial roads were close to new estates being built on the outskirts of the town and provided nuclei for gradually expanded suburban centres. This is what happened in one town: observation suggests that this 'natural' process may have occurred in many others.

But much of the expansion of suburban trade will take the form of the construction of new centres, such as Cowley, which has already been examined in a report published on behalf of the EDC[11]. If these centres are to succeed close attention must be paid to what are the requirements for success. These would appear to be:

1 *A complete range of convenience goods and a choice of trader for all these goods.* Shops like supermarkets and variety stores, which are in daily use, must necessarily form the nucleus of such a centre.

The range of other 'durable' shops depends on the relative functions of town centres and suburban centres.

Pavement surveys conducted by EDC staff at suburban centres in Redhill and Cowley revealed dissatisfaction on the part of shoppers with the range of shops present, especially with regard to the provision of clothes: either there were no ladies' clothing shops or they catered solely for one type of buyer. Women buy clothes fairly frequently and even more frequently like to 'window-shop' for prospective purchases. A lack of the right kind of shops may well drive them into town centres, so that the suburban centres will not be fulfilling their purpose. The lack of Marks and Spencers, British Home Stores, Littlewoods and department stores was also a cause of complaint. At present shops like these would not find it economic to set up in suburban centres, but they are shops that attract regular visits and their absence leaves a gap which may prevent a suburban centre from fulfilling its function. Part of the answer may lie with the development of 'junior' department stores* such as exist at Walton-on-Thames and Waterlooville.

2 *Sufficient support population to ensure a high level of prosperity and efficiency.* The Department of the Environment recommends thirty or forty thousand as the right size of support population but the circumstances of the town must be taken into consideration: for example where there are exceptional restrictions on the expansion of the town centre a suburban centre might have to cater for a larger proportion of consumers' expenditure than would otherwise be the case.

3 *Easier and quicker accessibility to the district centre from every part of the trading area than to any competing centre.* This includes accessibility by public transport, but this will not guarantee success in itself, as may be seen from the experience at Seacroft, Leeds, referred to in the previous chapter.

Many multiple shops have expressed the view that the setting up

---

* See Glossary

of a district centre of the larger type can only be justified where entry by road to the central shopping area is poor and cannot be improved. The sub-committee would reject this view: the strains imposed by traffic congestion within the central area must be taken into account as well.

The next three categories are marginal, and their share of total trade is likely to decline.

'Street-corner' shops

'Street-corner' shops are found in their thousands in the industrial areas of this country. They date back to an era when hours of work were long and mobility limited, and appear to have received a boost in the years of the great depression, when the wife would try to run a shop in her front room in order to feed the family while the husband was out of work. They mostly tended to become general shops selling a wide variety of types of goods but offering little or no choice within each type[12]. Many of these shops can hardly be called economic. It may well be that their social rôle is at least as important as their economic one: they provide the owner and local housewives with a point of social contact, as well as serving to supplement earnings or pensions derived from other employment.

The street-corner shop is typically found in working-class neighbourhoods, but now many of these neighbourhoods are to be razed in slum clearance programmes. Some local authorities have gone further and deliberately encouraged such shops to give up: in Portsmouth several score of shops have been closed in this way. We can hardly say that there will be no shops of this type in the 1980s, but given present trends it does appear that they will be of much less importance, though there will probably always be a place for some shops offering a high degree of personal service and, perhaps, open when other shops are closed, just as there will continue to be a certain type of person who prefers the independence and hazards of small shop-keeping to the discipline and security of being an employee.

Shops in intermediate areas adjacent to town centres

The difference between this category and the preceding one is that the shops are grouped together, are of more varied types and are rather more specialised. Usually, however, they are as old, although the factors affecting them may also affect new shops in intermediate areas.

We conducted a study of this type of area, as it appeared to be important. Our conclusions were as follows:

Factors conducive to the decay of such areas are:

1   *Changing patterns of trade.* A shorter working week and larger disposable income has meant that shops in central areas have become far more accessible and attractive: formerly intermediate shopping, often along radial roads, provided the only accessible shopping in a six-day working week. Now shoppers are accustomed to make regular weekly trips to central shopping areas for their 'durable' purchases and often for much of their 'convenience' shopping as well, leaving only a very limited amount of trade for shops in intermediate areas.

2 *Redistribution of population.* With more freedom of choice in housing, much of the hinterland population of the immediate areas has disappeared to the suburbs. Demolition of slums and mills has often accelerated this process, as in Doncaster, Preston and Bradford.

The re-distribution of population may not be as important as other changes in social patterns: at Preston, where slums have been replaced in one area of high density flats ten minutes walk away from the town centre, the small parade of five or six new shops at Kendal Lane has not been able to escape the general decline of older shops in intermediate areas.

3 *Redevelopment of town centres.* New developments in town centres have naturally acted as magnets to draw in an increasing proportion of trade. While empty shops may be found in new developments, decay is more likely to occur on the fringe of town centres, which are usually less attractive. Examples are found in Doncaster, Preston and Wolverhampton.

If a new development is itself on the periphery of a town centre it may itself be subject to this process, as is seen at the Main Square, Derby, and Waterdale (previously known as the Central Precinct) Doncaster.

4 *Demolition under road reconstruction programmes or slum clearance.* Demolition does not cause intermediate decay as such – it merely accelerates a natural process: for example, one reason for choosing a particular site for a road may be that the area is in decline already. However, the effect of the demolition sites on the character of an intermediate shopping area can lead to further decline. Examples of this can be seen in the radial roads at Preston and Doncaster, and at Wolverhampton.

There is some evidence to suggest that, particularly where there exists a high degree of overshopping in the town centre, demolition has been used selectively to destroy peripheral shopping. The ultimate aim here is to channel trade which might possibly have gone to peripheral shopping into the centre. An example of this was found at Doncaster.

5 *New roads.* These are often fast, wide relief roads with pedestrian barriers which can effectively sever pedestrian traffic between the town centre and intermediate shopping. The 'tightness' of ring roads varies greatly, the proposed Norwich scheme being an example of a 'loose' one (see Figure 7) and Chester a 'tight' one. But in either case intermediate shopping areas may be completely isolated from their natural hinterland population or cut off from the town centre on whose fringe pedestrian traffic they used to rely.

Many intermediate areas will automatically be superseded by central and district centres, but some shops found in them, such as spare parts shops and even second-hand furniture stores, provide a service to the consumer which is dependent on cheap sites and low overheads. Shortage of such sites has posed a problem in new towns (it arose, for example, in Basildon) and is likely to occur in other towns where large numbers of old shops are superseded by new shopping centres. The need for cheap sites of this kind could well be

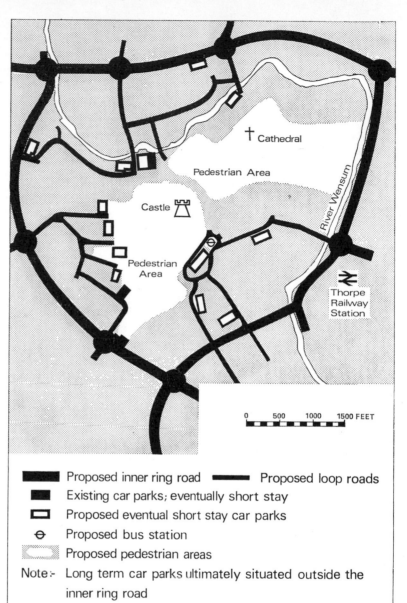

Figure 7
The ring road and
pedestrian areas proposed
at Norwich

Cathedral

Pedestrian Area

Castle

Pedestrian
Area

River Wensum

Thorpe
Railway
Station

0   500   1000   1500 FEET

Proposed inner ring road   Proposed loop roads
Existing car parks; eventually short stay
Proposed eventual short stay car parks
Proposed bus station
Proposed pedestrian areas
Note :- Long term car parks ultimately situated outside the
inner ring road

considered by local authorities: in some cases the need can be met, for example, by the provision of lock-up stalls in a covered market.

The problem of these intermediate areas may well be a passing one: once authorities have transformed their central areas they will perhaps turn to the 'inner ring'. It may well be that the intermediate areas will be devoted largely to housing, with the central shopping area surrounded by a belt free from shops. In this case the central shopping area could serve both as a local and a district shopping centre for a large population.

Parades of the type built in the 1930s

There is little to say of these. They are still built on estates, but are of decreasing importance overall. Much of the range of goods which they offer could probably be offered by a single small supermarket. It seems likely that goods outside a supermarket's range would probably be sought in a town or suburban centre anyway.

The share of trade of these three types of area has been declining since the war and many shops have already gone out of business. The conclusions stated in Chapter 3 suggest that the process of obsolescence may well be accelerated in the years to come, and this means that the businesses carried on in 'street-corner' shops and intermediate areas – and possibly in newer parades as well – will become increasingly marginal. These areas cannot be revived for shopping, and from a general planning point of view there does appear to be a need for urgent thought for their dedication to other uses: this is particularly relevant to the intermediate areas. There are obvious social problems as well that affect the people involved, but to suggest a solution to these would be outside the scope of this report.

Turning to the remaining types of development: 'Off-centre stores'* are just beginning to be acceptable to planning authorities, although doubts are still being expressed. But in dealing with free-standing superstores and out-of-town regional shopping centres we are entering a much more contentious area, and one where there is an urgent need for a definite view to be taken both by local and central government. It is in these areas that foreign experience is especially relevant.

Off-centre stores

This term covers a wide range of possible developments, but they have in common:

1   A limited range of goods
2   An off-centre location

They may go in for discount trading or they may be shops of an orthodox pattern taking advantage of low overhead costs to keep prices as low as possible.

Two examples of this kind of development may be cited.

The first is a chain of 'superstores' operating in the North of England. They are set up on a variety of different sites: some are in former factory buildings, others in purpose-built structures. Most are

---

* See Glossary

in 'off-centre' locations, one on a green field site. The one absolute necessity is plenty of room for car parking. They sell food and 'non-comparison durables' such as cheap clothes and shoes. The managing director alleges that he is definitely not trying to compete with town centres, the rôle of which he sees as catering essentially for comparison shopping. His experience of shops in new town developments is such that he feels that his shops can play their part just as effectively and at far less cost by choosing off-centre locations. The stores have a good image and the reaction of the local authorities, after an initial period of doubt, seems to be that they are to be welcomed.

The second example is a firm which has excited some comment in the national press because of its activities in Devon and Cornwall. The firm describes its developments as 'out-of-town shopping centres' and they are sited in former industrial buildings in rural locations. They deal in hardware, furnishing (including carpets) and clothing, but not food. Another example is a chain of discount stores in the North-West that set up in old industrial buildings and offer goods at cut prices both by buying up job lots and by leaving the shopper to break the bulk packages herself[13].

These two types of development aim essentially at the same thing and differ mainly in the acceptability of their image to local authorities, which depends largely on their regard for amenities, though it is worth noting that evidence has been produced to suggest that the discount type of store tends constantly to 'trade up', leaving a vacuum for an even more cut-price type of operation (which tends to 'trade up' in its turn)[14].

It is apparent that both types of store are serving the wants of a section of consumers at a low economic cost: it is for consideration whether they should not be encouraged, and brought within the planning framework, even though they may be resisted as 'unfair competition' by local and vested interest.

Free-standing superstores   One of the most significant developments in European retailing since the war has been the emergence of the superstore, sometimes called hypermarché or consumer market. Such stores usually have an aggressive pricing policy and almost always are free-standing, that is, not located in a new (or traditional) commercial centre.

In 1960 there were virtually no superstores in operation in Europe. In 1970 there are some 488 in operation, with a total selling space of 29 million square feet, and with parking for 285,000 cars. The countries where these stores have emerged most strongly are Germany, France, Belgium and Sweden. But they are now being opened in Switzerland, Austria, the Netherlands, Norway and Denmark. (See Appendix B and photographs.)

In the early years of development some of these superstores were summarily installed in vacant factories or warehouses with some parking facilities. Also there were few with over 50,000 square feet of selling space. But in the main period of growth to date, 1966 to 1970, the stores have been specially planned from the outset and the emphasis has been on size, up to 200,000 square feet of selling space, with parking lots for up to 1,500 cars. These superstores cater almost exclusively for the motorised shopper.

In addition to these superstores with a wide food and non-food assortment, a number of specialist retailers, particularly in the furniture trade, have opened very large free-standing stores surrounded by large parking lots: eg Ikea in Sweden and Denmark, and Möbel Pfister in Switzerland.

The superstore (offering discounts on durables) is also a major feature of American retailing, catering essentially for a car-borne population living in a suburban environment.

In this country Woolco are virtually the only exponents of this kind of operation, though other operators (notably Tesco and Carrefour) are studying this form of trading. Little hard information on the performance of Woolco is available as yet, but the Chairman of the parent company, F W Woolworth Ltd, has stated that experience to date has confirmed the Board's belief that these stores have a great development potential: sales during 1969 had exceeded their optimistic expectations[15].

There has been controversy over the best ways of managing such superstores: unified control and sub-contracting to licensees both have their protagonists abroad. It is not our purpose to comment on the relationship between operator and the licensee, although this can be critical, as was shown in the history of 'GEM'. What we are concerned with is the concept of a free-standing superstore – with many departments under one roof catering for the whole range of weekend shopping, supported by a number of specialist shops, and drawing customers from a very large area. So far the developments have been sited on the edge of conurbations. The response to our questionnaire seemed to indicate that this kind of shopping will be viewed favourably by the public, and it seems likely that given absolute freedom the number of developments of this kind would expand rapidly. American and European experience certainly reinforces this conclusion.

However, there does appear to be a certain amount of resistance from planning authorities, as may be seen from the abandonment of plans for developments of this kind outside Norwich and Southampton and at Murrayfield. Discussion with the parties concerned suggests that the main reason for this seems to have been a desire on the part of local authorities to protect the position of shops in central areas. The arguments against free-standing superstores have something in common with those against the establishment of regional out-of-town shopping centres, which we discuss below. It appears that, given present attitudes, the increase in numbers of stores of this type will be little, if at all, greater than it has been over the last few years, and it does not seem likely that the total number will be more than twenty: a more likely figure is about a dozen. If this is so, these stores may well make some impact on the trading patterns of individual towns, but it seems improbable that they would secure a significant proportion of national turnover.

We feel that local authorities are being too restrictive in their attitudes. Such evidence as there is suggests that these stores are both popular and efficient, and we would welcome a greater willingness on the part of the authorities to permit more to be built: they might, for example, be a satisfactory substitute for district centres in selected locations. In the event of such a change in policy we would anticipate a much greater increase in the number of stores of this type.

Out-of-town regional shopping centres

This major innovation in retailing originated in America, the first being the Country Club Plaza, Kansas, opened in 1923. The major expansion began to occur in the fifties: prior to 1950 only seven were opened, and by 1957 there were 160. By 1965 there were over 8,000, accounting for over a third of all retail sales in the US.

This class of centre provides all forms of general merchandise, clothing and furniture, and almost all the retail facilities available in the town centre. A population of at least 100,000 to 250,000 is needed to support such a centre, which can have a building area of well over one million square feet, the average being just over 400,000 square feet. The minimum site area is about 40 acres, with an average of 4,000 car spaces. About 45 per cent of the gross rentable area is occupied by department stores, who are the major lessees[16].

The main reasons for the development of out-of-town regional centres are:

1 *Increasing suburban population.* Between 1950 and 1960, the population of the USA increased by about 18 per cent[17]. The bulk of this increase is located in urban areas, but while the population of central areas increased by only 11 per cent, the increase in the major metropolitan suburbs was nearly 50 per cent.

2 *Increasing real income.* Between 1950 and 1966 real incomes rose by over 50 per cent[17] and the trend has continued. But since the more affluent have tended to move to suburban areas, the greatest increase in spending power has taken place there.

3 *Central area decay.* In many American cities there has been a marked deterioration of 'down-town' areas. The reasons are complex, and relate primarily to housing, but four factors are of importance:

(a) The general movement to the suburbs of the more affluent portions of the population, leaving the central areas to 'underprivileged' ethnic groups and 'poor whites' – both frequently immigrants from less privileged regions

(b) The tendency of retail trade to follow in the wake of purchasing power

(c) The inability of city governments to cope with the difficulties they face, arising from the local government structure which obtains and their frequently delicate position vis-à-vis State and Federal authorities – the history of Mayor Lindsay's administration in New York during the last few years is a case in point

(d) the decline of public transport.

4 *High level of car ownership.* Car ownership has developed to a level far higher than that obtained in Europe. In 1967, 78 per cent of all families in the USA owned cars, and about 25 per cent owned two

or more[17]. In many shopping centres 90 per cent of shoppers come by car.

A factor which facilitated the development of these centres was that large tracts of land could be cheaply obtained, especially at intersections between main roads and ring roads. Much of this construction has been undertaken in a laissez-faire fashion, with the result that newer centres are sometimes in direct competition with older ones.

In 1960 there were no large planned shopping centres in Europe coming within the definition of the Urban Land Institute*. In 1970 there are sixteen such centres with a gross leasable area of some 7.5 million square feet, a selling area of 5.5 million square feet, and parking for 45,000 cars. The centres are to be found in Belgium, Denmark, France, Germany, the Netherlands, Spain, Sweden and Switzerland. The more recent of these centres are two-level with a closed mall, and all of them have as 'magnets' either one or two department stores of over 35,000 square feet of selling space. Each of the sixteen centres has at least 200,000 square feet of selling space. (See Appendix B.)

Some of these shopping centres are located on 'green field' sites, some on the edge of towns, and some are surrounded by residential buildings. Nevertheless, the dominant characteristic of all these centres is that over three-quarters of the customers shop by motor car.

There are differences in conditions between Europe and the USA, in so far as it is possible to generalise. Many American centres are comparatively small (a quarter have less than 40 units[16]) and there are significant differences in the density of urban settlement, that in Europe being from two to ten times as high as in North America[18]. British conditions are more closely akin to those found on the Continent.

There is no true regional centre in this country at present. Haydock Park was the first site mooted, but planning permission was refused at all levels. Yate is regarded more realistically as a district centre – albeit a strong one – within the Bristol conurbation. Brent Cross (which took ten years to gain approval) can hardly be called 'out-of-town' although it may fulfil some of the functions envisaged by the Haydock Park type of centre.

This type of centre could be of great importance for the future, but the sub-committee is bound to report that it cannot offer a unanimous view. In the circumstances we feel that we will carry out our duty by stating the arguments for and against such centres.

The arguments *against* such developments are as follows:

1   The green belt or rural areas should be preserved at all costs. 'The problem of the out-of-town shopping centre is the problem of rigid planning restrictions affecting all buildings and development . . . The (regional) shopping centre for large industrial conurbations is the 'green belt' shopping centre and the green belt continues to be sacrosanct'[19]. Quite apart from the buildings themselves, the

very large expanses of car park required are alleged to be destructive of amenities.

2 Diversion of trade to out-of-town regional shopping centres would imperil the urban renewal programme of sizeable industrial centres and might 'kill' trade in smaller towns. Discussions with a number of planning officers suggest that the programme of investment in many town centres has gone too far to be reversed, and that those concerned with municipal planning would view with grave disquiet any development which would channel off a substantial proportion of the consumer spending which was reckoned on, either explicitly or implicitly, when the development programmes were started. There are relatively few town centres where the available shopping space cannot at present be extended by one means or another, whatever the implications for the future, and it would seem likely that towns prefer to invest in district shopping centres within their boundaries rather than 'out-of-town' centres outside them.

An illustration of this point of view is provided by one local planning authority's arguments against the establishment of an out-of-town centre of this type[20]. In the view of the planning authority:

'The marginal reduction in road problems caused by the removal of some shopping traffic from cities and towns would in no appreciable way reduce the need for public expenditure on relief and service roads, car parks and numerous other facilities.

'This development would reduce that element of private investment which, when associated with public investment, allows substantial redevelopment and is largely the means of making these traffic and other improvements physically and financially possible.

'Since the development of larger and competitive shopping units is bringing about a rapid decline in the numbers of small shops and Board of Trade estimates indicate that this should continue, a situation which would remove trade from these towns, would accelerate the closing of shops within them and the further decline of the urban fabric of these towns'.

Now, this comment relates to an area of industrial towns which have in some respects been declining and where an injection of capital is urgently needed in order to maintain the quality of urban life. To this extent it is a special case – but it is a case which relates to many of the conurbations in this country, and probably most of those outside the South-East of England.

Loss of trade was quantitatively estimated by a team at Manchester University when investigating the Haydock Park proposals: in their report it was estimated that Liverpool, Manchester and Bolton would lose about 12 per cent of their actual trade in 1971, and that Warrington would lose 46 per cent, Wigan 41 per cent and St Helens 34 per cent[21]. It was for this reason, as well as for traffic considerations, that the application to build Haydock Park development was refused.

The main arguments *for* out-of-town regional centres are as follows:

1 While the 'green belt' argument has force it must be recognised that the 'green belt' is often far from green, littered as it frequently is with derelict army camps, disused railway marshalling yards,

abandoned mills and quarries and the remaining detritus of a decaying industrial age. Where such sites are suitably placed in relation to centres of population and the road system serving them, development for shopping would improve amenities, not destroy them.

2   It is said that towns in the UK are so much closer than they are in the USA and space will never be available except in rural areas where there is no spending power. But the essential difference between the USA and the United Kingdom cannot be explained by reference to either the proportion of the population living in conurbations or the density of towns within metropolitan areas. Extra-urban centres are found even in metropolitan areas of the USA where the density of towns can reasonably be compared to the density of towns in the United Kingdom, and the proportion of the American population living in conurbations (46 per cent) is not very different from the proportion of the British population living in conurbations (47.5 per cent). (The American definition of a standard metropolitan statistical area[17] has been adopted in each case, although the above comparison probably understates the British percentage.) The bulk of the American population does not live in isolated towns on a featureless plain. This being so, an appeal to American experience and the behaviour of car-borne shoppers in the USA is relevant. European experience is, *a fortiori*, even more relevant, as the pattern and density of settlement in all West European countries, including ours, is very similar.

3   Out-of-town regional centres cater specifically for shoppers with cars who do not wish to shop in town centres. Such centres are an accepted feature of retailing in other countries with a comparable standard of living, and consumers in this country are deprived of a legitimate choice if such centres are not built: in the absence of such planned centres they may seek substitutes and encourage the growth of unplanned centres in aircraft hangars and the like, or overstrain the shopping resources of country towns and villages (as may be seen round Norwich at present).

In the absence of an agreed view, we believe that the arguments summarised above express fairly the main points on each side. Three additional considerations are perhaps relevant:

1   The main arguments on either side stem from entirely different 'philosophies': one places more value on choice being offered to the consumer and more trust on market forces securing a good allocation of resources, whereas the other emphasises the social necessity of preserving the quality of life in towns.

2   The argument that town centres should be preserved is on the face of it an extremely cogent one, but it does rest to a large extent on assertion rather than ascertainable fact. More detailed cost benefit analysis of this subject is required.

3   The impression is widely held that the authorities are opposed, on grounds either of principle or of unwillingness to accept radical changes, to the concept of out-or-town regional shopping centres. If central government is not opposed in principle, it would be of great

assistance to all parties if clear guide lines were to be published indicating under what circumstances regional out-of-town shopping centres would be regarded as acceptable or desirable.

References

[1] Ministry of Transport, *Traffic in Towns,* HMSO, 1963

[2] A M Tulpule, 'Forecasts of vehicles and traffic in Great Britain', Road Research Laboratory, Ministry of Transport, 1969

[3] G Sternlieb, *The Case of American Cities,* paper given to conference *Urbanisme et Commerce,* Stockholm, 1969

[4] J Vrebos, 'Public transportation versus city highways, the Belgian experiment', paper given to conference *Urbanisme et Commerce,* Stockholm, 1969

[5] B Millbom, 'Metropolitan Railways in Stockholm', paper given to conference *Urbanisme et Commerce,* Stockholm, 1969

[6] L H Jacobsen, 'Modern public transportation in the Netherlands', paper given to conference *Urbanisme et Commerce,* Stockholm, 1969

[7] Llewellyn-Davies, Weeks, Forester-Walker and Bor, *Milton Keynes Plan; Interim report to the Milton Keynes Development Corporation,* 1968

[8] G Bohman, 'Present and Future Problems in commercial city planning', paper given to conference *Urbanisme et Commerce,* Stockholm, 1969

[9] D Owens, *Parking: a survey of some parking standards adopted by county boroughs in England and Wales,* Road Research Laboratory, Ministry of Transport, 1968

[10] *The Intermediate Areas: Report of a Committee under the Chairmanship of Sir Joseph Hunt,* Cmnd 3998, HMSO, 1969

[11] Distributive Trades EDC, *The Cowley Shopping Centre,* HMSO, 1968

[12] Union of Shop, Distributive and Allied Workers, *Report on the Planning and Control exercised by local authorities over the number and location of retail shops,* March 1967

[13] *The Grocer,* August 9, 1969

[14] E Agergard, P A Olsen, J Alpass, 'The interaction between retailing and the urban centre structure: a theory of spiral movement', *Environment and Planning,* Vol 2, No 1, 1970

[15] F W Woolworth & Co, *Annual Report,* 1969

[16] C S Jones, *Regional Shopping Centres: their location, planning and design,* Business Books, 1969

[17] US Department of Commerce, Bureau of the Census, *Statistical Abstract of the United States,* 1968

[18] M Dix, 'Commercial and Shopping Centres in Germany', paper given to conference *Urbanisme et Commerce,* Stockholm, 1969

[19] N A M Stacy and A Wilson, *The Changing Pattern of Distribution,* Pergamon, 1958 and 1965

[20] West Riding County Council, *Proof of the Local Planning Authority: Appeal against non determination of proposed shopping development at Carlinghow Lane, Batley,* December 1969

[21] Manchester University, *Regional Shopping Centres in North West England,* Part One, 1964

Chapter 7 The structure of planning

In this chapter we wish to draw together the conclusions arising from the previous chapters and consider them in relation to the general planning structure existing in this country. Consideration will be given to the structure itself, then to the powers possessed by local authorities.

The structure

In examining the planning structure, it is important to define the essential problems facing planners. This was stated in the report of our Models Working Group[1].

'It has to be appreciated that for predictable reasons, there are going to be substantial new developments in the pattern and capacity of shopping in the next ten to twenty years. There will be population growth and population redistribution, not only by growth of established towns and cities but also by the creation of new settlements. Redressing of regional imbalance could increase the disposable income per head of the poorer regions relative to the rest of the country, and local transformation of accessibility through new road works will change the pattern of shopping. There will probably be a continuation of trends in central area dispersal although central area renewal will still be an important factor, and will to some extent counteract this trend. Nonetheless, it should be borne in mind that despite the rate and scale of new developments, there is likely to be considerable rigidity in the basic framework now existing. The changes that are likely to take place in shopping over the next ten or twenty years are only marginal within the established context.

'Even so far as these changes are not changes in the shopping system itself, they are certainly changes in the environment in which the shopping system exists. Thus the forecasts should not simply amount to what the market would do, but must be influenced by the local authorities' development plans and the Government's decisions on regional studies. For this reason a starting point could be a summary assessment by Government Departments concerned (particularly the Department of the Environment and the Department of Trade and Industry) of their official local and regional plans in so far as they affect shopping.

'Within this general approach, we need to differentiate between various problem situations on the ground, since different approaches will be required for different sizes and locations of shopping centres.

'A breakdown of problems by hierarchy is useful in this respect, for two reasons. Firstly, government decision-making in planning is hierarchical; there is interaction between central government, regional organisation and two- or one-tier local government – for example, even though a local authority is responsible for London or Manchester, these centres must also be considered at the national and regional level by central government. Secondly, a problem often relates to the particular centre and the approach to its solution will be affected by its position in the hierarchy. Here we are not only concerned with the effect of centres of equal rank, but the much more complex question of how much trade the higher and lower order centres will take – for example, the district centre problem in the new town. Hence it is not often that one can say that a problem is concerned with only one level of hierarchy: the problem will nearly always span a number of levels, though not necessarily all levels'.

This implies that the planning structure must be adapted to the fact that retailing is carried out in a hierarchy of shopping centres (see Figure 8) with dependent areas of widely varying sizes and populations (to envisage this one might compare Manchester, Bolton and Huyton and the way they draw customers in respect of different types of goods). The problem is complicated by the fact that the shopping hierarchy is not the only one to be considered:

Figure 8 The hierarchical pattern of shopping centres in England and Wales, 1961

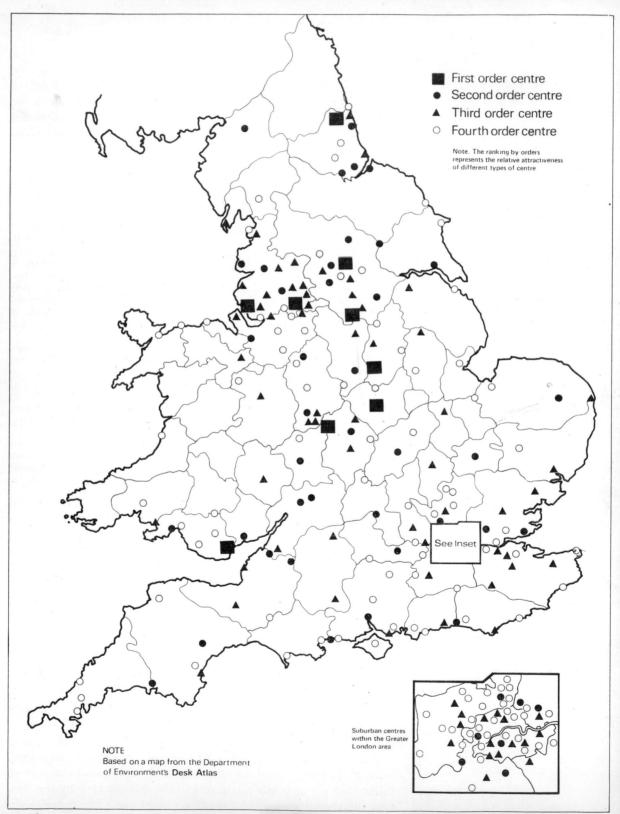

■ First order centre
● Second order centre
▲ Third order centre
○ Fourth order centre

Note. The ranking by orders represents the relative attractiveness of different types of centre

See Inset

Suburban centres within the Greater London area

NOTE
Based on a map from the Department of Environment's **Desk Atlas**

'The retail hierarchy should have some affinity with other hierarchies such as education, the welfare services and recreation since there are many possibilities for the joint use of facilities, particularly transportation'.[2]

The hierarchical nature of the network of shopping centres which exists in the country leads to two important conclusions about the planning structure which is desirable.

Firstly, it implies that decisions on shopping provision should be taken at an appropriate level and should recognise the differences both of scale and kind between a regional centre and a small town or suburb.

Secondly, it implies that there should be full interplay between central, regional and local planning, following 'an iterative process whereby higher level decisions will influence lower level decisions, but in turn be influenced by the more detailed study which is made at the lower levels. This implies that higher level problems would be studied at a greater degree of generalisation than the lower levels, for the precision in type of decision required is necessarily much less'.[1]

The present structure of local government creates a number of difficulties as regards the overall provision of shopping. Many of the important shopping centres are county boroughs – but the boundaries of the planning authority in almost all cases sever the town from much of its trade area. County planning authorities operate over a much wider area but are not responsible for the major towns, and in any case are too small to conduct planning on the large regional scale. The regional planning councils have done some valuable work in the examination of needs and of existing trends, but they are not executive bodies.

Local government powers The Town and Country Planning Act of 1968 imposes on each planning authority the duty of preparing a structure plan*. The Act provides that so far as shopping is concerned, this plan will be able:

1 To set out the policy and general proposals relating to the hierarchy of centres, the growth in town centres, the creation of new centres, the development of district centres and the relief of congestion in town centres.
2 To deal with the quantity of floorspace at significant stages and its distribution.
3 To lay out the broad criteria and policies for the location of new development, subsequent local plans, development control, and existing development in relation to conservation and conversion.
4 To deal with priorities and phasing, particularly in relation to action areas, and to deal with implementation such as the assembly of sites by local authorities and the scope for private development.

These structure plans will require the approval of the Secretary of State for the Environment, who will be responsible for co-ordinating the strategy.

* See Glossary

Current planning legislation also lays down responsibility for the approval of individual shopping developments.

If a local authority proposes to deal with an area by way of comprehensive redevelopment, this requires confirmation by the Minister and he must be satisfied as to the amount and location of shopping proposed in consequence of the redevelopment. Compulsory powers may or may not be sought but as owners of land within the area of comprehensive development, the local authority will be able to control the development not only as planning authority but also as the landlord, and under present legislation the terms of the proposal have to be approved by the Minister.

It is in regard to other developments that the picture is not so clear. Very broadly, assuming that a proposed development is in an area zoned so as to permit commercial building, a local authority still has adequate powers to refuse planning permission for a development on grounds which include the fact that too much traffic congestion will be created and that local shopping capacity is being built beyond the demands of the neighbourhood. But if permission is refused the developers can appeal to the Minister (who can also 'call in' important proposals – a power comparatively infrequently exercised). There are some grounds for thinking that in the past local planning authorities have been chary of using their veto powers because they are nervous of having their decisions exposed to a critical examination by experts at a public enquiry: this nervousness may have nothing to do with the merits or demerits of the decision they are defending. Another, possibly more cogent, reason is that local authorities have taken the view in the past that where a private developer was prepared to invest large sums of money on shop development within a town centre, it was not for the planning authority to question the success of the centre. There is, in fact, a strong temptation to come to an arrangement with the developers. The instances of considerable over-provision encountered during the sub-committee's work, at Doncaster and Derby, were private developments, and this over-provision was not anticipated by the local authorities in their scrutiny of the proposals.

It would appear that the planning structure as laid down by existing legislation is adequate to deal with the problems involved in shopping development. The fact that errors have been made in the past would seem to arise from the way the system has been operated rather than from the nature of the system itself. In particular we would wish to make the following comments.

1 Although the Department has the responsibility of considering the structure plans of individual planning authorities in the way outlined above, and of co-ordinating them, it has made no public statement of national or regional planning strategy in respect of shopping provision. Such a statement would be of material assistance to all those involved in or affected by the planning process.

2 Shopping, and the provision of the buildings which cater for it, is a dynamically changing process, but considerable inertia has been imposed on the shopping process since in many cases major developments have taken several years to secure approval (in the

case of Brent Cross as long as ten years). Under the old procedure planning authorities prepared development plans (inevitably a lengthy process in itself) and the Department took years to approve them. In view of the importance of shopping and the waste of resources that may result from delay, we urge that the new legislation should be operated in such a manner as to secure speedy decisions regarding development plans and applications for development.

3 There has been insufficient co-ordination by the central authority of neighbouring planning authorities' policies: we have encountered a number of instances where the scale of concurrent developments in neighbouring towns seems likely to lead to over-provision.

4 Regional shopping strategy must be adequately developed: from our point of view it is immaterial whether this function is carried out by regional planning councils, by provincial councils (as proposed in the Maud Report[3]) or by the Department itself, so long as it is carried out effectively.

5 At the local level, we would stress the need for planning authorities to examine not only the physical nature but also the economic viability of shopping proposals, their effect on other developments and the changes in the pattern of trade which would result if approval were forthcoming. It is natural that a local authority should desire to secure modern, large and successful developments in its town, but there may well be dangers of over-provision in relation to competing centres: a local authority may not be in the best position to appreciate them, and this suggests that review at a higher level may be desirable.

The question of local authorities acting as developers on their own account and of the relationship between local authorities and developers, may also be considered here.

If a local authority wishes to develop a shopping centre on a site it usually acts by means of a developer with whom it comes to a financial arrangement. There have, however, been a number of cases where local authorities have acted as developers and landlords on their own account. While the view has been expressed that local authorities are in a less favourable position with respect to their capital position[4] – a view with which we would not wholly agree – we have come across instances of lack of commercial expertise in the letting and running of shopping centres developed by a local authority. This is a job for professionals in this particular field, and it is essential that local authorities should get the best possible advice, and if necessary employ the best possible agents, if they are to compete on level terms with successful property developers, who acquire very considerable expertise from their operations in all parts of the country.

A number of cases where precincts had failed seemed to have arisen from the fact that the contractual relationship between local authority and developer was less than ideal. Two instances were when the site had been auctioned (the Town Hall site, Preston and the Waterdale precinct at Doncaster). In other cases the site had been put out to tender. In confining its responsibility to gaining the maximum price for a site, a local authority may put the developer who makes the top bid in a position where he must either build an unjustifiably large number of shops or try to get very high rents, or both, in order to recoup his outlay. However, it is fair to say that the normal procedure by now is a partnership between a local authority and a development company[5], and it is extremely unlikely that any of the major development companies would wish to operate in any other way: this method is the only one where real co-operation is likely. It is essential in these cases that a good brief should be prepared on the basis of an adequate shopping study: this brief should safeguard non-financial considerations and must be considered in relation to the regional planning framework.

The cogency of our recommendations in this chapter is underlined by the possibility, given present trends, of some over-provision of shopping floorspace by 1980. If there are too many shops, or too much shopping capacity, this could mean a waste of sites, and a waste of resources. Such a risk justifies the most careful operation of the planning mechanism.

The planning strategy should not take account only of the total amount of floorspace required. We have suggested that while the proportion of trade in town centres is likely to change little, the proportion carried on in suburban centres will increase, and the proportion carried on in other locations will diminish. This implies that there must be a consistent policy of developing suburban sites and also that consideration should be given to the shops which present trends will render increasingly marginal: as we have pointed out in the previous chapter many of these will be in locations adjacent to town centres or on 'street-corner' sites in the old residential areas of industrial towns. Particular attention should be paid to the social and planning problems resulting from the accelerating obsolescence of shops in these locations.

The Department of the Environment should lay down guide lines stating criteria for the acceptability of free-standing super-stores and out-of-town regional centres: rightly or wrongly, the impression is widely held that planning authorities are apt to discourage both forms of development on principle. Such guidance, based on analysis of the costs involved, both financial and social, would be of great help to all those concerned with planning for the provision of shops.

To sum up, we would conclude that present legislation is adequate to deal with the problems involved in shopping development, though local authority boundaries create some difficulties. Such criticisms as we have concern the way the system is operated, with particular reference to delays in decision and the development of regional shopping strategy. In part, these criticisms stem from the fact that insufficient attention has been paid by government to shopping in the past: we examine this question further in the last chapter.

References   1 Models Working Party *Urban Models in Shopping Studies,* NEDO 1970
2 D Diamond, 'Provision of commercial facilities', *Grangemouth-Falkirk Regional Survey and Plan,* Vol 1, Chapter 3, HMSO, 1968
3 *Report of the Royal Commission on Local Government,* Cmnd 4040, HMSO, 1969
4 A Likierman and A Wilcock, 'Suburban shopping precincts – an assessment', *Journal of the Town Planning Institute,* Vol 56 No 4, April 1970
5 The Hammerson Group of Companies, *Hammersons in the United Kingdom,* 1969

Chapter 8 The importance of work on shopping capacity

In the course of the sub-committee's work we have found it evident that in many respects we were breaking new ground. This is not to say that a considerable body of knowledge does not exist – the list of projects in Appendix A is evidence of this – but much of the work deals with specific problems, being variously conducted by town planners, geographers, economists and representatives of other disciplines. There is little or no co-ordination of this research, neither does the study of shopping facilities receive the same attention as, for example, that of transport facilities.

This is disturbing: consumers' spending in shops accounts for nearly one-third of the gross domestic product and shop staff account for more than one worker in every twelve in the country*. The EDC has already emphasised distribution's rôle in the economy[1]. It points out that a more efficient distribution system will reduce the cost of living, since distribution costs (including transport, whole-saling and advertising) must account for nearly half the cost of consumer goods to the shopper.

'In the UK retail trade in 1968 there were approximately:

> 540,000 shops (owned by about 300,000 separate organisa-tions)
> 2,600,000 people working in them
> £12,000,000,000 of sales
> £1,400,000,000 of stocks, at cost
> £220,000,000 of fixed investment was probably made last year.'

The lack of *organised* research on shopping capacity surely reflects the low priority which government has attached to distribution, both retail and wholesale, and also the low priority retail distributors have attached to the development of their own industry as a whole. An instructive comparison may be made with transport economics, which has a somewhat similar degree of importance in the national economy. Transport economics is a highly organised discipline, and this is due in no small degree to the interest and encouragement of the former Ministry of Transport, to which it was a major concern. But the study of shopping provision is not co-ordinated in any way, there being at present no body responsible for taking a synoptic view of the research undertaken: this, we would suspect, is at least in part because the provision of shops is only one of many concerns of the Department of the Environment, of the Department of Trade and Industry which is the sponsor department for distribution, and of the Ministry of Agriculture, Fisheries and Food, which has an interest in food distribution.

---

* This figure relates to employees in employment

The tentative nature of many of our conclusions reflects and emphasises the need for organisation and encouragement of more studies in this field. If the subject is to be studied in a properly co-ordinated way a continuing body should be set up. This might be under the aegis of a government department (as is the Road Research Laboratory) or a university (as is the Institute of Manpower Studies) or an institution working in a closely allied field (like the Institute for Food Distribution or the Centre for Environmental Studies). An interesting model for such a body could be the Institute of Centre Planning in Denmark. This was set up by retailers and the co-operative movement. The Institute originally received support from the Government: now, however, it operates without a government grant and virtually all of its revenue is derived from payments for contract work. The Institute is of interest because it has played a significant part in developing retail studies in Denmark at a small cost to the public purse and also because its constitution permits it, as it would not permit a body run by a government department, to preserve absolute independence vis-à-vis all parties, including the Government. Since its inception bodies with a similar aim have been set up in other continental countries, notably Sweden and France.

We would stress to all those concerned in this field – to retailers, property developers and consumers, as well as to central and local government – the great need for such an institution devoted specifically to the quantitative and qualitative study of shopping provision. The continued lack of such a co-ordinating body will suggest that retailing, and particularly the provision of shops of a high standard, holds an undeservedly low place in the community's list of priorities, and that the use of vast resources by the retail trade is likely to continue to be less efficient and economic than it could be.

Reference   [1] EDC for the Distributive Trades, *Distribution Efficiency and Government Policies*, NEDO, 1969

Glossary of terms

While every effort has been made to write the report in non-technical language, some terms which may be unfamiliar or which have special meanings in a retailing context have had to be used.

Central shopping areas The main shopping centres of larger towns, characterised by the presence of department stores or other large shops attracting shoppers from a wide area. The method of demarcation is described in full in the published volumes of the Census of Distribution for 1961.

Free-standing superstore For the purpose of this report this is defined as a large retail unit, with at least 25,000 square feet of selling area, situated outside the conventional commercial centres and located on the edge of or outside a town. Food and non-food goods are sold by self-service, and the store is surrounded by large parking facilities.

Grocery sales Sales of food not made by specialist food retailers, ie dairymen, butchers, fishmongers, greengrocers, bakers and off-licences.

Gross floorspace The whole of the superficial area occupied by the retail business, ie including stockrooms etc, as opposed to *nett floorspace* which refers only to the selling area to which the public has access.

Independent retailers Retailing organisations having less than ten branches.

'Junior' department stores A small department store, usually in a suburban location and commonly offering a reduced number of merchandise categories.

Multiples Retailing organisations having ten or more branches.

Off-centre store For the purpose of this report, this is defined as a retailing unit, of between 10,000 and 25,000 square feet, situated outside a central or suburban shopping area and provided with substantial parking facilities. Such a store may sell food or non-food goods, or both.

Out-of-town regional shopping centre In North America such a centre is defined as a shopping centre situated outside the built-up area of a town, providing all forms of general merchandise, clothing and furniture, and almost all the retail facilities available in a town centre. A population of at least 100,000 to 250,000 is required to support such a centre, which varies in building area from 400,000 square feet upwards. The minimum site area is about 40 acres, with an average of 4,000 car spaces. The centre contains at least one department store.

Parking standard The amount of car parking accommodation available to serve given area of retail floor space: it may be measured as parking s per 1,000 square feet gross floorspace.

Planned shopping centre   A group of commercial establishments planned, developed, owned and managed as a unit, the centre having a planned mix of tenants in relation to the market served and in almost all cases providing on-site parking for customers.

Punched card retailing   A form of retailing in which the shopper makes her choice from the items on display by selecting a punched card for each item she wishes to buy. The cards are handed in at the check-out and a delivery note is made out automatically at the same time as the bill is added up. The goods are then packed by staff and subsequently collected by the customer.

Shopping capacity   The total amount of retail floorspace available.

Structure plan   A plan submitted for ministerial approval – primarily a written statement of policy, accompanied by a diagrammatic structure map for counties and major towns only, designed to expose clearly the broad basic pattern of development and the transport system. Such structure plans form the main link between policies on a national and regional level and local planning, and indicate 'action areas', ie areas where comprehensive development, redevelopment and/or improvement is envisaged in the ten years after submission.

Superette   A self-service food shop of between 2,000 and 4,000 square feet nett floorspace.

Supermarket   A self-service shop of over 4,000 square feet nett floorspace: such shops sell food predominantly, but the larger ones may sell an increasing range of non-food items.

Appendix A Research into problems allied with shopping capacity

The following list covers all the research projects known to the Office at June, 1970, and is mainly based on the registers published by the Institute of Food Distribution, the Town Planning Institute and the Social Science Research Council. While every effort has been made to ensure that the list is as comprehensive as possible, we cannot guarantee that some individual projects of interest to the sub-committee have not been omitted. If this is so, apologies are offered to the individuals and institutions concerned.

Belfast, Queens University of – Department of Geography
Spatial groupings of shops – function and form (MA thesis).

Birmingham University – Centre for Urban and Regional Studies
The planning process and the development of new communities–5-year project 1967–72.

Birmingham University – Department of Geography
Towns in the Midlands: a study of service centres with special reference to the conurbation.
An identification of the central place hierarchy in the Midlands as a whole and within the West Midland conurbation. G M Lomas.
Publication: G M Lomas, 'Retail trading centres in the Midlands', *Journal of the Town Planning Institute,* March, 1964.

Bristol City Council – Planning Department
Offices in Shopping Centres, 1967.
Results of a survey of nine different-sized shopping centres to find the characteristics of non-shopping commercial uses. Five main groups have been identified, and employment, spheres of influence, travel to work and car-parking characteristics are being studied in each case.

Development Analysis Limited
1 *Evaluation of land-use demand for shopping*
This study includes the application of a gravity potential model and the calculation of turnover/sq ft ratios.
Publication: T Rhodes and R A Whitaker, 'Forecasting shopping demand', *Journal of the Town Planning Institute,* May 1967.

2 *Shopping survey for Torbay CB*
3 *Quantitative model of market shares and location factors in store development*
A mathematical model developed to give retailers a basis for determining market shares in new locations and calculating optimum

store size, based on a systematic analysis of the locational and other factors determining market shares in existing locations.

Publications: *Shopping in Redbridge;*

Selected Sites in Shopping Centres, paper by R W Evely given to International Study Conference, *Opportunities in retailing,* September 1969; *Estimating Shopping Requirements: Concept and Practice in Great Britain,* paper by R W Evely to International Symposium on *Planning of trade networks in conditions of European cities,* Prague, 1969.

Durham University – Department of Geography, Distributive Trades Research Unit

1   *Major suburban shopping centres – their potential and impact*

Phase one: A general survey of the location, size and form of new suburban shopping centres in all areas of Great Britain (not at present available in an organised and comprehensive form).

Phase two: An analysis of selected centres before and after development, in order to provide information about their operational impact.

2   *Inter-regional and inter-urban variation in retailing in Great Britain*

(a)   A geographical study of retail trade and business districts in English country towns, with an examination of regional and urban variations.

(b)   A study of the locational and structural characteristics of main shopping centres in Great Britain.

Publication: D Thorpe, 'The main shopping centres of Great Britain, their locational and structural characteristics', *Urban Studies,* Vol 5, No 2, 1968.

3   *Shopping centres and trading areas*

Elements of this research have been studies of:

(a)   Supermarket catchment areas: work on their characteristics and implications for future planning.

(b)   Shopping centres and customer movement: analysis of the relationship between shopping centres' size and attractiveness at various distances.

(c)   Trading areas of department stores in North East England.

Publications: D Thorpe and T C Rhodes, 'The Shopping Centres of the Tyneside Urban Region and large-scale Grocery Retailing', *Economic Geography,* Vol 42, 1966;

D Thorpe and G A Nader, 'Customer Movement and Shopping Centre Structure', *Regional Studies,* Vol 2, 1967.

Glasgow University – Department of Social and Economic Research

Economic and social determination of planning standards, 1967–70

A study of the determinants of land use change, with particular emphasis on the use planners make of planning inducements and controls. The efficacy of a range of other 'weapons' is being studied.

GLC Planning Department

Assessment and projection of requirements for shopping floorspace
Based on London sample of *The Family Expenditure Survey* in 1961–64
and on *Land Use Survey* results.

Hull University – Department of Geography

Central place studies in East Yorkshire 1966

Keele University – Department of Geography

A study of central places in Staffordshire and Shropshire 1967

Kent County Council – Planning Department

The influence of car ownership on shopping habits 1964

Lanchester College of Technology – Department of Town
Planning

1   *Variable relationships in shopping models*

The project examines the suitability of various data inputs in both
central place and retail potential models, with special reference to
the use of raw Census data rather than specific indices based on
field work or special computations. Attention is also being given to
the effectiveness of various disaggregated gravity models at local
levels of forecasting.

Publications: R L Davies, 'A note on Centrality and Population Size', *The
Professional Geographer*, March 1969;

R L Davies, *Variable Relationships in Central Place and Retail Potential Models,* Regional
Studies;

R L Davies, 'Effects of Consumer Income Differences on Shopping Movement
Behaviour', *Tijdschrift voor Economische En Sociale Geographie,* Vol 60, 1969.

R L Davies and B J Styles (ed), *Gravity Models,* Lanchester College, 1969.

2   *Space preferences in intra-urban shopping behaviour*

This study is concerned to identify functional sub-systems of consumer behaviour within the Coventry shopping hierarchy. Patterns
of movement between shopping centres, linkages between shops
visited and underlying motivations for consumer preferences are
being investigated according to social class reference groups.

Leeds City Council – City Engineers' Department

The pattern of shopping in the city in relation to turnover
A major study of suburban shops to obtain a hierarchy of shopping
centres.

Leeds University – Department of Civil Engineering

Traffic generation of retail department stores

Leeds University – Department of Geography

1   *The extent and processes of urban renewal in the central areas of towns
and cities in West Yorkshire in the post-war period*
Examines urban renewal in nine West Riding towns. The floorspace
index prepared in 1949 has been used to define the past functional

character of the central area and how this has been modified by redevelopment. 1965–68 PhD thesis.

2 *The functions and grading of rural service centres in part of East Yorkshire*

Leicester University – Department of Economics

Retail trade patterns in the East Midlands

The project is concerned with examining retail centre catchment areas and in making estimates of future retail sales in the various East Midland retail shopping centres. Two techniques in particular are being used, a gravity model and principle component analysis to aid the classification of retail shopping centres.

London School of Economics – Department of Geography

1 *Retail consequences of office expansion in Central London*

An investigation of the impact on retail location and retail sales of office expansion in central London.

2 *The geography of retailing*

An account of the factors affecting the distribution of shops with particular reference to ways the pattern has changed since 1945 and will change up to 1985. Special attention is being paid to forecasting suitable for town planning purposes.

London School of Economics – Social Science and Administration Department

Study of town expansion schemes 1967–71

London University: Queen Mary College – Department of Geography

Aspects of the urban hierarchy in England and Wales

London University: University College – Department of Town Planning

The growth and changing function of urban centres in South London 1801–1961

An analysis of the physical, economic and social factors affecting the location of central place functions in South London. Topological analysis is being used to determine:

1 The centrality of service centres

2 The extent to which this reflects the connectivity of the local and regional network

3 The extent to which centrality has influenced the growth and regional status of industrial service centres

The changing economic base characteristics of South London boroughs is examined in the light of current and proposed town planning policies.

Publication: M P Collins, 'A Study of urban complexes within the South half of the Greater London Region' in *Report of the Royal Commission on Local Government in Greater London 1957–1960*, Vol 5 – minutes of evidence.

Luton College of Technology – Department of Science

Shopping habits and shopping centres in South Bedfordshire

The influence of Luton on rural districts in South Bedfordshire and adjacent areas, with special reference to shopping habits, assessed by means of a questionnaire seeking to find out where the rural population shops for various goods and by what means of transport, and also by means of a survey of the area to examine the distribution of shops.

Manchester University – Centre for Urban and Regional Research

1 *Shopping gravity models – a better measure of centre attractiveness*

Sponsored by Ministry of Transport

Part of a programme of research directed at improving the effectiveness of the shopping gravity model concept as a planning and productive tool. The research examines ways of assessing the attractiveness of shopping centres to shoppers in order to find which measures may be used most effectively to predict shopping trip patterns to these centres, and is based largely on the Stoke-on-Trent area.

2 *An urban simulation model*

An investigation of shopping activities of people in the Manchester area. The impact of parking restrictions on shops, and the behaviour of car shoppers in Central Manchester. Part of a larger long-term project to produce a model into which any data on any town may be fed, to predict likely consequences of proposed changes in land use, traffic policy etc. New models to interpret urban phenomena will be evolved as part of the research programme.

Publications to date: D F Medhurst and J Parry Lewis, *Urban Decay*, Macmillan, 1969;
Occasional paper No 1, 'Measured Techniques in Planning, No 1: Linear Programming';
Occasional paper No 2, 'Measured Techniques in Planning, No 2: Cost Benefit Analysis'.

3 *Control of urban and regional systems 1969–71*

The application of cybernetic principles to the design, implementation and review of plans for towns and regions, including a fundamental study of theories of control in highly complex systems with examples of practice drawn from a sample of British planning authorities.

Ministry of Housing

Major shopping centres in England and Wales

Publication: W I Carruthers, 'Major Shopping Centres in England and Wales 1961', *Journal of Regional Studies Association*, May 1967.

Newcastle upon Tyne University – Department of Geography

Changing distribution of service provision in major centres of North-East England

Newcastle upon Tyne University – Department of Town and Country Planning

The economics of town centre redevelopment – M Litt Thesis 1966–69

Norfolk County Council – Planning Department

Town centre costing

This study probed methods of assessing total capital cost and returns in long-term central area plans for small market towns, and the annual rate charge on the basis of acquisition, clearance and construction costs and ground returns only.

Oxford University – Institute of Agricultural Economics

The economics of small towns and rural centres

Oxford University – Nuffield College

1   *A study of Cowley shopping centre*

This study analyses the social background of the people who shop at Cowley and their reasons for doing so.

Publication: *The Cowley Shopping Centre*, HMSO, 1968.

2   *The effects of changes in the location of shops and the introduction of new shops on consumers' behaviour: a case study of Oxford*

Reading University – Department of Estate Management

Value and analysis in shopping areas

A comparative study of value patterns and the interpretation of value gradients; examination of the relationship between rental and turnover.

Reading University – Department of Geography

Classification and ranking of towns as service centres; their spheres of influence and regionalisation in Southern England

Sheffield University – Department of Geography

Central place studies, with special reference to Wales 1966

Strathclyde University – Department of Economics

Redevelopment of shopping centres

Three reports to local authorities concerned on the redevelopment of shopping centres at Clydebank, Motherwell and St George's Cross, Glasgow. The reports were conducted by the Scottish Development Advisory Group.

Strathclyde University – Department of Geography

1   *Retail facilities and shopping patterns of Glasgow*

This comprehensive investigation involves the distribution of different types of shop, including the analysis of confirmations and the subsequent examination through questionnaires of shopping affinity patterns in selected areas.

2   *Retail facilities and shopping patterns in Ayrshire*

Surrey County Council – Planning Department

Shopping potential in Surrey

Sussex University – Department of Geography

Intra-urban spending flows

For each of 93 zones in the Sussex coast conurbation were calculated:

1   Zonal spending power, distributed between five main spending categories.

2   Zonal turnover in each of these categories as assessed by a complete field survey of 8,000 retail outlets.

The data was used to draw up maps showing contoured surfaces relating to each of five commodity groupings, and inferences were drawn about optimal location of various new facilities.

Sussex University – Geography Laboratory

Dynamic pressures on the Crawley sub-region

To assist the County Council in preparing an overall plan for the area the pressures for growth in Crawley and the surrounding area were investigated and the restraints to development assumed. The researchers carried out a series of retail surveys in several towns in the area and evaluated the likely growth in retail sales within the area. This was published as part of the *Crawley Expansion Survey* by the West Sussex County Council Planning Department.

Sussex University – School of Social Study (Geography Division)

Dynamic aspects of service provision and population structure in the central place system of south eastern England

An examination of the interaction of component status variables (social structure, price/range and rank); exogenous or endogenous input variables and resultant output variables (consumer behaviour change in central place rank for the basic elements of consumers, commodities and central places).

Wales, University of, University College, Aberystwyth – Department of Geography

1   *The hierarchy of commercial centres: a case study in South Wales 1964*

2   *Investigations into the urban geography of Wales*

An investigation of the distribution and physical characteristics of Welsh towns.

Publication: H Carter, *The Towns of Wales:* a study in urban geography 1965.

Wales, University of, University College, Swansea – Department of Geography

1   *Comparative study of central place systems*

This involves studies of the urban hierarchy and the trade area of towns mainly in South Wales but also in the Southampton region, South Yorkshire and Pennsylvania.

Publications: W K D Davies, 'Some Considerations of Scale in Central Place Analysis', *Tijdschrift Voor Economische En Sociale Geografie,* Vol 56, Nov/Dec 1965;
W K D Davies, 'Centrality and the Central Place Hierarchy', *Urban Studies,* Vol 4, Feb 1967;
W K D Davies, 'Ranking of Service Centres: a critical review', *Transactions and papers of the Institute of British Geographers,* Vol 40, Dec 1966;

W K D Davies and G W S Robinson, 'The nodal Structure of the Solent Region', *Journal of the Town Planning Institute*, January 1968.

2 *Space relations of communities: migration, journey to shop and to work*

Publication: W K D Davies, 'Latest migration potential and space preferences', *Professional Geographer*, Vol 18, 1966.

3 *Techniques of analysis of central places and the application of the results to administrative boundary re-organisation*

Yorkshire and Humberside Planning Region

Regional Shopping Study

Appendix B Data on new developments in Europe

The following tables present data on some of the principal new shopping developments that have taken place in Western Europe in the last few years, with particular reference to the construction of large 'out-of-town' regional centres existing to serve a largely car-borne population.

Table B1 Estimates of the number of self-service shops and super-markets in Europe

Table B2 Superstores in Europe

Table B3 Specification of Parly 2 shopping centre

Table B4 Wertkauf superstore

Table B5 Examples of large shopping centres in Europe

Table B6 Selling space in European countries

Table B1 Estimates of the number of self-service shops and supermarkets in Europe 1 January, 1970

Country	No of self-service units	of which supermarkets
Austria	5,700	60
Belgium	2,700	400
Denmark	5,500	150
Finland	3,000	120
France	19,400	1,130
Germany	84,700	1,880
Ireland	1,000	40
Italy	2,900	310
Netherlands	9,000	350
Norway	4,000	100
Spain	5,000	100
Sweden	8,500	850
Switzerland	5,000	280
United Kingdom	28,000	1,300
Total	184,400	7,070

Total selling space in self-service shops can be estimated at 210 m sq ft, of which 37 m sq ft is in supermarkets of 4,000 sq ft or more selling space.

Note: The self-service and supermarket units in department stores, variety stores and superstores are excluded. Most of these units, *c.* 2,100, would be classed as supermarkets.

Source: International Association of Department Stores

Table B2 Superstores in Europe 1 January, 1970

Country	No	Selling space '000 sq ft	Parking places
Germany	368	21,750	180,000
France	73	4,300	72,000
Belgium	15	1,140	9,300
Sweden	10	805	12,900
United Kingdom	6	315	5,200
Others*	16	675	7,000
Total Europe	488	28,985	285,400

* Austria (10), Netherlands (3), Switzerland, Norway, Denmark (1 each)
The data relate only to stores with 25,000 sq ft of selling space or more

Table B3 Specification of Parly 2 shopping centre (see photograph)

Location	Le Chesnay, 13 miles West of Paris, 2½ miles north of Versailles.

The centre is in the middle of the Parly 2 housing estate consisting of 36 apartment houses, with some 5,000 flats. The whole estate, including the shopping centre, tennis courts, swimming pools, church, schools, etc, covers just over 200 acres. This centre is the first of 15 planned around Paris in the next ten years.

Responsibility for development Private enterprise with reluctant agreement by the Greater Paris authorities.

The shopping centre Two-level, enclosed, air-conditioned mall with 120 different retailers and services, including restaurants. The total gross leasable area is some 575,000 sq ft and selling space about 400,000 sq ft.
The largest units are:

	Selling space sq ft
Printemps, department store	112,000
BHV, department store	80,000
Prisunic, variety store	30,000
Suma, supermarket	17,000

Parking Parking for 3,000 cars: a large motor centre with car-wash, etc soon to be installed.

Opening hours

Mondays and Saturdays 10.00–20.00 hrs
Tuesday to Friday 11.00–22.00 hrs
The mall, restaurants and bars open all day including Sunday to 23.00 hrs.

Promotions The centre has a monthly newspaper and promotions in the mall change every week.

Zone of attraction area

	No of inhabitants (actual)
Living in area	20,000
5 minutes by car	50,000
10–15 minutes by car	400,000

In 1980 the potential market is expected to be 650,000.
It is expected that 90 per cent of the customers will go to the centre by motor car.

Sales Estimate for first year £21,500,000, of which the department stores took about one-third.

Table B4 Description of Wertkauf superstore, near Karlsruhe

Location	At the Durlach motor-way interchange some 3 miles from the centre of Karlsruhe.
Size	180,000 sq ft of selling space on one level, of which 20,000 sq ft a food supermarket.
Employment	450 persons. Personnel costs 5–6 per cent of sales.
Selling method	Complete self-service, 34 check-outs, 20 fitting rooms for women's ready-to-wear. Certain departments are operated by concessionaires; watches, jewellery, furs, photographic goods. books. Payment is made in the department in these cases.
Other services	The centre also includes cafeteria, hairdressing for men and women, dry-cleaning, pharmacy, pet shop, a building materials centre and a garden centre.
Parking	2,000 cars. Also petrol station and automatic car wash. 400 tyres changed daily, 80–90 per cent of customers come by car.
Cost	Total cost, including land, *c.* £3–5 million.

Table B5: Details of some shopping centres in Europe

Centre	Near	Km distance from city centre	Date opened	Total commercial space '000 sq ft	Estimated retail selling space '000 sq ft	Department stores No	Department stores Selling space '000 sq ft	No of parking places	No of levels	Closed or open mall	No of parking places per '000 sq ft commercial space
Skärholmen	Stockholm	12	1968	600	450	2	116	4,000	1	O	6.7
Ruhrpark-Einkaufszentrum	Bochum	9	1964	580	440	2	120	4,000	1	O	6.9
Main-Taunus-Zentrum	Frankfurt	10	1964	570	420	2	195	5,000	1	O	8.8
Parly-2	Paris	19	1969	590	400	2	180	3,000	2	C	5.1
Rijswijk	The Hague	4	1966	460	350	2	120	2,300	1	O	5.0
Frölunda Torg	Gothenburg	7	1967	550	350	2	95	3,000	3	C	5.4
CAP 3000	Nice	6	1969	500	300	1	150	3,500	2	C	7.0
Täby-Centrum	Stockholm	12	1968	470	300	2	75	1,800	2	C	3.8
Nordwestzentrum	Frankfurt	8	1968	370	290	2	160	2,300	2	O	6.2
Woluwé	Brussels	7	1968	370	310	2	150	1,700	2	C	4.6
Elbe-Einkaufszentrum	Hamburg	12	1966	330	240	2	100	2,500	1	O	7.6
Spreitenbach	Zürich	14	1970	350	250	2	92	1,600	2	C	4.6
Rødovre	Copenhagen	10	1966	400	200	1	25	1,600	2	C	4.0
Donau-Einkaufszentrum	Regensburg	2	1967	250	180	2	90	2,000	2	C	8.0

Note: Total commercial space is the gross leasable area of all retail and service establishments. Malls etc are excluded.

Table B6: Selling space in some European countries

Country	Source and date	No of Establish-ments	Estimated selling space million sq ft	Average selling space per establish-ment sq ft	No of inhabitants per 10 sq ft selling space
Belgium	Census 1961	160,000	65.0	400	1.4
Norway	Census 1963	34,000	19.9	590	1.8
Sweden	Census 1963	53,840	44.2	820	1.7
Switzerland	Census 1965	51,800	37.9	730	1.6
W. Germany	Beckermann 1965	na	302.9	na	1.9
France	CICOD 1965	na	300.0*	na	1.6
UK	Jefferys 1966	520,000	335.0	640	1.7
Netherlands	Bak 1968	145,000	76.0	520	1.7
Finland	Central Statistical Office 1968	37,685	25.1	670	1.9
Italy	Ministry of Industry and Commerce 1969	835,400	335.2	400	1.6

* Including service establishments
na = not available

In the German Democratic Republic the 1967 Census showed 48.2 million sq ft of selling space in 110,254 establishments.

Using the data set out in the above table as a base, it can be estimated that there are some 3,400,000–3,500,000 fixed retail establishments in the eighteen countries of Western Europe, and these establishments have a selling space of 1,700–1,800 million sq ft. This suggests some 500 sq ft per establishment and 1.9 inhabitants per 10 sq ft of selling space.

In the past decade, for the first time, a number of European countries included questions in their Censuses of Distribution on the selling space of retail establishments. At the same time, a number of experts in other countries have made estimates of selling space. The data for ten European countries is given in Table B6.

It should be stressed, however, that the Census figures in many cases have had to be re-calculated to allow for non-response. And an attempt has been made to make the figures comparable, so butchers and bakers are included in retail establishments, but petrol stations and motor vehicle dealers are excluded. In most cases, kiosks are also excluded and, of course, all non-fixed retailers, market stalls, etc.

Appendix C Future pattern of retailing questionnaire

This appendix contains the results of an exercise that was undertaken in the first place because the sub-committee needed to know what might happen in a number of fields which were important for the consideration of how much shopping capacity should be provided in the 1980s, and of what kind. The fact that existing data are not up to date nor sufficiently reliable precluded reliance solely on projection techniques. A working party was therefore set up to formulate a questionnaire dealing with these problems, to decide to whom it should be sent, and to advise on the analysis of results.

The method used was to try to find out what the consensus of opinion was among various interested parties (retailers, planners, property developers, consumers and so on) by sending out a postal questionnaire. Two rounds of the questionnaire were circulated, the second permitting some modification of the original answers.

The numbers in the groups approached, and the degree of response, is indicated in Table C1. Two points should be made about the respondents: firstly, they replied as individuals, or on behalf of individual firms, and not as members of an executive body of a trade association; secondly, with regard to the retailers, although relatively few in numbers their firms represented a much higher proportion of national turnover than their numbers would indicate.

Table C1: Respondents to the two rounds

	No receiving questionnaire	First round replies	Second round replies
Co-operative societies	30	14	9
Multiple shops	24	11	7
National Chamber of Trade	30	14	7
Retail Alliance	24	17	13
Retail Distributive Association	16	5	5
Total retailing groups	124	61	41
Planning officers	48	21	20
Property developers	12	5	1
Economic development consultants	10	2	1
Academics	25	9	5
Mail order firms	9	2	1
Voluntary groups	9	5	4
Food manufacturers	14	9	8
Consumers	16	8	1
Others	8	2	1
Total	275	124	84

Summary of replies 1 Respondents anticipated that the total number of shops would drop by about 10 per cent by 1975 and a further 10 per cent by 1980, a final total of 400,000 shops.

2 Respondents forecast that in 1975 the share of total trade held by department stores would remain constant at 5 per cent, that the share held by multiples would rise from 32 per cent to 39 per cent, and that the co-operatives' share would fall from 9 per cent to 8 per cent. Mail order would rise from 4 per cent to 6 per cent (a view which the Sub-Committee would treat with caution, as American and European experience suggests a ceiling of 5 per cent). Independent retailers' share would fall from 50 per cent to 41 per cent. The same trends were expected to continue till 1980.

3 The most important factors enabling the independents to play a continuing part were expected to be personal service, specialisation and voluntary groups.

4 Voluntary groups were expected to grow most in hardware and pharmacy, in textiles and in electrical goods.

5 Grocery outlets (including supermarkets) were expected to increase their share of the total food trade from 40 per cent in 1961 to 49 per cent in 1975 and 53 per cent in 1980, specialist food shops (ie butchers, bakers and greengrocers) would fall from 39 per cent in 1961 to 33 per cent in 1975 and 30 per cent in 1980. The share of co-operatives was expected to drop slightly and the sale of food in non-food shops to rise.

6 The number of self-service shops was expected to rise from 22,000 in 1969 to 28,000 in 1975. Their share of grocery trade would rise from 57 per cent to 70 per cent in 1975, and of all food trade from 24 per cent now to 35 per cent in 1975. The bulk of this increase would not take place in the small self-service shops but in supermarkets of 2,000 sq ft upwards and especially in the largest supermarkets of over 10,000 sq ft selling space. This last group is anticipated to quadruple in numbers to 400 by 1980, with its share of grocery trade rising from 4 per cent to 15 per cent, of all food trade from 2 per cent to 9 per cent.

7 For non-food sales, it was expected that the share of specialist shops (eg clothing shops, shoe shops and ironmongers) would drop from 75 per cent in 1961 to 70 per cent in 1975 and 65 per cent in 1980, that of department and variety stores would rise from 23 per cent in 1961 to 25 per cent in 1975 and 28 per cent in 1980 and that of food shops (including supermarkets) would rise from 2 per cent in 1961 to 5 per cent in 1975 and $6\frac{1}{2}$ per cent in 1980.

8 Of possible new methods of retailing, it was thought that private customers shopping in cash and carry warehouses would be the most significant development (especially for food, but also for non-food). Telephone ordering was also likely to be important. Other factors mentioned were punched card retailing and automatic vending but these were not thought likely to be important.

9 The majority view was that as consumers' income rose the amount of food bought would be the same, but at greater unit prices. For durable goods, most thought that both greater quantities and goods of higher value would be bought.

10 The general impression was that if shopping hours were extended this would be by means of opening at least some evenings during the week, although there was a substantial minority that anticipated seven-day opening of supermarkets and, to a lesser degree, of other food shops.

However, comments generally suggested that an extensive alteration of shop hours might prove uneconomic and impracticable. In response to a question enquiring about the times people would shop most respondents answered that they thought people would shop mostly at weekends – few anticipated much evening shopping.

11 It was envisaged that between now and 1980 there would be a marked increase in the share of total trade held by suburban shopping areas, which would be the main point of expansion. This would be partly at the expense of central shopping areas but mainly at the expense of isolated shops, village shops and small 'parades'. Free-standing superstores might go up from less than 1 per cent to 3 per cent and regional shopping centres – non-existent at present – might take 2 per cent of the total turnover. The general consensus was that large free-standing superstores had more of a future than regional shopping centres.

12 It was anticipated that new planned shopping areas in existing shopping centres would meet with a favourable response, though obviously this would depend on the quality and layout of individual developments. The most important single planning factors to be taken into account were parking and general accessibility, followed by good social amenities, good pedestrian flow, attractive appearance and environment. A good variety of shops was held to be very important, and also the presence and good siting of 'magnet' stores. An adequate support population was also important.

13 Respondents were of the opinion that future developments in central shopping locations would be multi-storey and elsewhere single-storey.

14 They were also agreed that consumers and developers would view covered centres with favour, and that retailers would be at least neutral.

15 They were agreed that provision should be made for shops of different sizes by using modular construction in developments, so permitting flexibility in division, to meet lessees' reasonable requirements, or by consulting lessees before development takes place, or by a combination of both (they are not, of course, incompatible): there was little support for the alternative of forecasting what percentage of shops would be of predetermined sizes and shapes and building accordingly.

16 It is estimated that 10 to 12 per cent of all journeys made to different types of shopping centre are made by car. Respondents expected this proportion to more than double by 1980. The Sub-Committee considered that the figures were of importance in the estimation of necessary parking provision. A question regarding standards of parking provision suggested 6 spaces per 1,000 sq ft of shopping space would be needed in central shopping areas in 1980, 5 in suburban centres and $8\frac{1}{2}$ in out-of-town centres.

Appendix D Calculation of consumers' expenditure in 1980

Consumers' expenditure was estimated by the Department of Applied Economics at Cambridge, the broad outline of the method being as follows (see Wigley[1], for details). Consumers' expenditure was broken down into nine categories: motor cars; furniture; radio, television and electrical goods; food (including drink and tobacco); clothing and footwear; miscellaneous household goods; housing; fuel and light; transport and services. Tables were made of consumers' expenditure under these headings for the years 1958 to 1969, at 1963 current prices, using Tables 24 and 25 of the National Income Blue Book 1969. The figures were worked out as expenditure per head of population, as it had been found that the models used fitted better to this kind of data than to overall expenditure.

The first three categories were treated separately from the other six: expenditure on these 'durable' goods represents a small but variable element in consumers' expenditure and is thus worthy of special treatment. Year to year changes in expenditure on these goods were accounted for by means of capital stock adjustment models, in which the desired stock is a function of the level of real income (modified by a scrapping term and a term standing proxy for credit restrictions) so that changes in price have effect on purchasing decisions for durable goods through their effect on real incomes. This model does not take account of any changes in the relative price of durable and non-durable goods which does not affect real income*.

In the case of the remaining six categories the linear expenditure system was fitted to the data. This system (see J R N Stone[2]) expresses expenditures in each category as a linear function of (a) total expenditure and (b) category prices: it should be noted that it takes account simultaneously of changes in both factors in calculating their effect on the structure of consumer spending.

The following basic assumptions were made:

1 Two values of the annual growth of GDP were assumed – a 'high' one of 3.75 per cent per annum and a 'low' one of 2.75 per cent per annum from a base year of 1969.

---

* The ultimate equation was

$$\Delta 1_t = \sigma ak + \sigma b \Delta \delta_t + \sigma bk \delta_t - \sigma 1_t - c \Delta \xi_t$$

where in the year t, 1_t is real investment per head of population in the commodity concerned, δ_t is real disposable income per head (and $\Delta \delta_t$ is the increment in this in the year t) and $\Delta \xi_t$ is a measure of changes in the proportion of down payment required for hire purchase. σ, a, b, c and k are unknown parameters to be estimated.

The elasticity of the desired stock with respect to real disposable income is calculated as

$$\eta_t^* = \frac{b \delta_t}{a + b \delta_t}$$

Since a is usually negative and b positive this elasticity is positive and greater than unity, but for large values of disposable income tends to unity.

2 The proportion of GDP represented by consumers' expenditure would remain constant at the 1969 figure of 63.6 per cent. It could be argued that the faster rate of growth of GDP would require a switch of resources into investment. A possible consequence would be a lower share of GDP available for consumption. This possibility has been ignored in the calculations because its effect is negligible compared to the differences between the two rates of growth assumed.

3 Food prices (excluding prices of drink and tobacco) would rise by 15 per cent in relation to the prices of manufactured goods if either the UK entered the Common Market under present agricultural arrangement or the agricultural support policy was abandoned for other reasons. It is assumed that the relative prices of these other commodities do not change. The rise of 15 per cent in the food price is lower than the figure of 18–20 per cent given in the White Paper 'Britain and the European Communities: an Economic Assessment'[3] but this admits that this is the most that is likely to occur, and the 15 per cent estimate represents the consensus of the opinions of a number of other authorities (for instance the CBI[4]), though it does assume some alteration of the Common Market agricultural pricing policy. With regard to this assumption two extreme cases are considered:

(a) that *money* incomes will be fully compensated (by increased government transfers to persons, family allowances, old age pensions etc, or reductions in direct taxation) so that *real* incomes are maintained: in this case expenditures on durable goods, which are assumed to be a function of real income, are unaltered, or

(b) that *money* incomes remain unchanged so that *real* incomes fall by the full amount of the price rise and, in addition, expenditure on durable goods falls.

These two cases are headed 'B' and 'C' respectively in Tables D1 and D2 and may be termed the compensated and uncompensated cases. It should be stressed that neither case, and especially the compensated case, is likely to occur in practice, and that what actually will happen will be somewhere between the two limits, but the two cases represent extremes bracketing the likely outcome of the assumptions made.

Estimates were made for 1975 and 1980 and take account of the effects of the 1967 devaluation. While only 1980 figures were necessary for the purposes of this report, it was felt that the 1975 figures were interesting in themselves and had the added advantage that they could be compared with other published estimates.

Estimated figures of consumers' expenditure, broken down among the nine categories, are given in Tables D1a and D1b (for 1975) and Tables D2a and D2b (for 1980). For each year six estimates are given, the first series (in the top half of the table) assuming a 'low' growth rate of 2.75 per cent per annum and the second series (in the bottom half) assuming a 'high' growth rate of 3.75 per cent per annum. The 'A' projections assume no relative charge in food prices (ie they assume no entry into the Common Market); the

'B' and 'C' projections assume a rise in food prices of 15 per cent (eg arising from entry to the Common Market), representing the compensated and uncompensated cases respectively.

It should be noted that a direct comparison between the 'A' projection on the one hand and the 'B' and 'C' columns on the other should not be used to suggest that real expenditure on food will necessarily drop as a result of entry to EEC. Chapter III of the White Paper[3] suggests that this might lead to acceleration of the rate of national production and real income: this could easily more than compensate for the relatively small drop in real expenditure on food forecast at *fixed* growth rates of GDP.

Table D1a: Projections of consumers' expenditure for 1975 with low rate of growth in real GDP of 2.75 per cent pa
(£m at 1963 prices)

	Basic food price		Food price + 15%		
	Price indices (1963=1.000)	Pro-jection A1	Price indices (1963=1.000)	Pro-jection B1	Pro-jection C1
Motor cars etc	—	1,303	—	1,303	1,199
Furniture etc	—	646	—	646	623
Radio, electrical etc	—	698	—	698	663
Food, drink, tobacco	1.534	8,255	1.685	8,113	8,011
Clothing, footwear	1.322	2,445	1.322	2,460	2,391
Misc household goods	1.498	2,389	1.498	2,405	2,330
Housing	1.730	3,041	1.730	3,076	2,907
Fuel and light	1.419	1,419	1.419	1,433	1,369
Transport and services	1.568	6,423	1.568	6,485	6,186
Total		26,619		26,619	25,679

Table D1b: Projections of consumers' expenditure for 1975 with high rate of growth in real GDP of 3.75 per cent pa
(£m at 1963 prices)

	Basic food price		Food price + 15%		
	Price indices (1963=1.000)	Pro-jection A2	Price indices (1963=1.000)	Pro-jection B2	Pro-jection C2
Motor cars etc	—	1,499	—	1,499	1,389
Furniture etc	—	686	—	686	663
Radio, electrical etc.	—	755	—	755	721
Food, drink, tobacco	1.534	8,442	1.685	8,287	8,180
Clothing, footwear	1.322	2,559	1.322	2,575	2,504
Misc household goods	1.498	2,513	1.498	2,530	2,453
Housing	1.730	3,319	1.730	3,358	3,185
Fuel and light	1.419	1,524	1.419	1,539	1,474
Transport and services	1.568	6,915	1.568	6,983	6,678
Total		28,212		28,212	27,247

Table D2a: Projections of consumers' expenditure for 1980 with low rate of growth in real GDP of 2.75 per cent pa (£m at 1963 prices)

	Basic food price		Food price + 15%		
	Price indices (1963=1.000)	Pro-jection A3	Price indices (1963=1.000)	Pro-jection B3	Pro-jection C3
Motor cars etc	—	1,673	—	1,673	1,578
Furniture etc	—	738	—	738	721
Radio, electrical etc	—	828	—	828	798
Food, drink, tobacco	1.705	8,907	1.856	8,749	8,645
Clothing, footwear	1.417	2,809	1.417	2,826	2,756
Misc. household goods	1.648	2,736	1.648	2,754	2,680
Housing	2.030	3,532	2.030	3,570	3,414
Fuel and light	1.569	1,687	1.569	1,702	1,640
Transport and services	1.762	7,575	1.762	7,645	7,357
Total		30,485		30,485	29,589

Table D2b: Projections of consumers' expenditure for 1980 with high rate of growth in real GDP of 3.75 per cent pa (£m at 1963 prices)

	Basic food price		Food price + 15%		
	Price indices (1963=1.000)	Pro-jection A4	Price indices (1963=1.000)	Pro-jection B4	Pro-jection C4
Motor cars etc	—	2,084	—	2,084	1,971
Furniture etc	—	823	—	828	804
Radio, electrical etc	—	953	—	953	917
Food, drink, tobacco	1.705	9,308	1.856	9,121	9,016
Clothing, footwear	1.417	3,067	1.417	3,087	3,014
Misc. household goods	1.648	3,008	1.648	3,029	2,952
Housing	2.030	4,109	2.030	4,154	3,990
Fuel and light	1.569	1,917	1.569	1,935	1,869
Transport and services	1.762	8,639	1.762	8,722	8,420
Total		33,913		33,913	32,953

The estimates for 1975 were compared with those from other sources known to us[5][6] and found to be very similar, though not necessarily in detail.

Of the nine categories, those relevant to the planning of shopping capacity were: furniture etc; radio, television and electrical goods; food, drink and tobacco and miscellaneous household goods. Much alcoholic drink and tobacco is sold otherwise than through retail outlets (eg in public houses, restaurants etc). The trends in these sales do not appear to have been studied authoritatively, but calculations on figures available to the Office suggest that in 1980 a proportion of about 20 per cent should be deducted from the food, drink and tobacco category to allow for sales through non-retail outlets.

Sales of other commodities through non-retail outlets must also be allowed for. The major form of trading to be considered here is mail order. On the basis of replies to our questionnaire on the future pattern of retailing we would estimate that the share of mail order in total trade would be about 5 per cent in 1980. This figure therefore needs to be deducted from the total figure.

Consumer expenditure in shops is therefore estimated to be as shown in Table D3.

Table D3: Estimated consumers' expenditure in shops, 1980
(£m at 1963 prices)

	2.75 per cent growth in GDP			3.75 per cent growth in GDP		
	Basic food price	Food price up 15 per cent		Basic food price	Food price up 15 per cent	
		Real incomes constant	Money incomes constant		Real incomes constant	Money incomes constant
Food, drink, tobacco	7,126	6,999	6,816	7,446	7,297	7,213
Clothing and footwear	2,809	2,826	2,756	3,067	3,087	3,014
Furniture	738	738	721	828	828	804
Radio/TV/ electrical	828	828	798	953	953	917
Miscellaneous household goods	2,736	2,754	2,680	3,008	3,029	2,952
Total	14,237	14,145	13,771	15,302	15,191	14,900
Less 5 per cent	712	707	688	765	759	745
Total expenditure in shops	13,525	13,438	13,083	14,537	14,432	14,245

In calculating the total shopping floorspace required in 1980, we are interested mainly in the extreme cases and the value falling half-way between them, ie a high extreme of £14,537 million represented by the high growth rate, basic food price case, a low estimate of £13,038 million (the low growth rate uncompensated case) and a middle value of £13,810 million.

In assessing shopping needs it is further necessary to consider shifts in the general pattern of spending. This may be considered most conveniently by examining the percentage of total expenditure represented by each of the categories of consumers' expenditure forecast by the model and comparing it with current figures, as taken from the current National Expenditure Blue Book (see Table D4).

Table D4 Per cent consumers' expenditure in various categories 1968 and 1980 (estimated)

	1968	Est 1980 (low extreme)	Est 1980 (high extreme)
Food, alcohol, tobacco	33.4	29.3	27.3
Clothing etc	8.9	9.4	9.0
Furniture	2.2	2.4	2.4
Radio/TV/electrical	2.4	2.7	2.8
Miscellaneous household goods	9.1	9.1	8.9
Motor cars	4.2	5.3	6.1
Housing	11.2	11.6	12.1
Fuel and light	5.1	5.2	5.7
Transport and services	23.5	25.0	25.4

These figures suggest that the proportion of money income spent on furniture will rise slightly, on clothing, radio, and on TV and electrical goods quite significantly; there will also be marked rises on housing and motor cars. On the other hand the proportion of income spent on food will fall significantly and that spent on 'miscellaneous household goods' (which include soft furnishings, hardware, cleaning materials, reading matter, and recreational goods) will remain about the same.

There is some corroborative evidence on this matter.

Tipping[7] has used Family Expenditure Survey data to calculate the percentage distribution of household expenditure for various percentiles of the distribution of household income in the years 1959,

Table D5 Percentage distribution of household expenditures for certain percentiles of the distribution of household incomes 1959–65

	Percentile				
	5th	25th	50th	75th	95th
Food	36.3	34.2	32.7	29.1	24.3
Alcohol	1.9	2.9	3.2	3.8	4.7
Tobacco	3.6	6.3	6.7	5.9	5.0
Total food, alcohol and tobacco	41.8	43.4	42.6	38.8	34.0
Housing	17.8	12.1	10.8	9.6	8.5
Fuel and light	13.5	8.5	6.6	5.5	4.3
Durable household goods	3.6	5.9	6.5	6.8	7.3
Clothing and footwear	5.9	8.4	8.9	10.1	11.3
Transport and vehicles	3.1	6.7	9.1	12.5	12.7
Miscellaneous goods	6.8	7.3	7.4	7.8	7.9
Services	7.2	7.6	7.9	8.6	13.8
Total*	99.7	99.9	99.8	99.7	99.8

* Each reading is an average of four interpolated values. The total of the ten such averages is unlikely to give exactly 100 per cent

1962, 1963 and 1965. Table D5 gives the average of these results (the 5th percentile is near, if not below, the poverty line; the 95th percentile is relatively wealthy).

If one treats this analysis as if it were a dynamic one, by imagining that one was looking at changes in real income through time instead of through a range of incomes, then – considering the retail groups only – by 1980 there would be a *relative* drop in the amount spent on food, drink and tobacco and a *relative* rise in the amount spent on clothing, durable household goods (including furniture and radio, TV and electrical) and miscellaneous goods.

It should be stressed that this approach is limited in two ways: it can only be used to demonstrate indications of the *direction* in which the proportions of different categories move, not their absolute dimensions; also, it considers only income elasticities, and not price

Table D6 Demand elasticities for various commodity groups

	Prais and Houthakker[8][9]		Beckerman[10]	Stone and Rowe[11]
	I	E	E	I
Farinaceous products	.47	.33		
Dairy products	.36	.26		
Vegetables	.55	.40		
Fruit	.75	.55		
Meat	.60	.44		
Food			.26	.52
Beer			.26	
Other alcoholic drinks				.52
Tobacco				.83
Drink and tobacco			.74	
Footwear				1.60
Other clothing				1.65
Clothing and footwear	1.35	1.24	1.57	
Furniture				1.76
Durable household goods				2.21
Hardware				2.36
All durables	1.94	1.77		
Household expenses			1.05	
Literary	1.36	1.05		
Rent	.83	.49		
Fuel and light	.95	.73		—.05
Vice	.78	.61		
Communications			.27	
Transport			2.48	
Entertainment			—.40	.33
Other			2.02	

* Series marked I are income elasticities. Those marked E are expenditure elasticities

elasticities. The assumed 15 per cent rise in food prices in the 'low' case given in Table D3 obviously affects to a considerable degree the conclusions which would be drawn purely from an examination of income elasticities.

Another way of approaching the problem is by examining the income and expenditure elasticities for various commodity groups. It should be borne in mind that any figure representing elasticity is a relative figure dependent on the method of calculation, not an absolute figure, so that elasticities of some items published by different authorities using different methods are not comparable: what is important is the relative dimensions of different categories in each series. A summary of a number of post-war calculations is given in Table D6.

This is not the place to discuss the methodologies of the several authorities: these are given in the references cited and in Q Paris[12].

The general picture is, however, the same in all these analyses: there is agreement that the elasticity of food, drink and tobacco as a whole, is less than unity (implying for these items a progressively smaller part of increasing real income and expenditure provided that there is no change in the relative prices of the several categories), and that other goods, including clothing, furniture, hardware etc will account for a progressively greater part of total expenditure. This agrees reasonably well with the conclusions reached from examination of Tipping's tables[7]: it should be noted that these conclusions also are based on income and expenditure elasticities only. It should be noted that the effects of *both* price and income changes are taken into account in the DAE analysis.

Conclusion

On the whole the evidence suggests that the pattern of expenditure will tend to shift away from food, drink and tobacco (as a whole: 'other alcoholic drink' is an exception) towards other goods; this shift will be more marked if this country did not enter the Common Market than if it did, because of the relatively higher price of food.

References

1   K J Wigley, to be published
2   J R N Stone, 'Models for Demand Projections' published in *Essays on Econometrics and Planning*, Pergamon, 1965
3   *Britain and the European Communities: an Economic Assessment*, Cmnd 4289, HMSO 1970
4   Confederation of British Industry: *Britain in Europe*, 1969
5   R Brech, unpublished paper
6   J Tanburn, *People, Shops and the 70s*, Lintas Special Projects, 1970
7   D G Tipping, 'Price Changes and Income Distribution' *Applied Statistics*, 19 No 1, 1970
8   S Y Prais and M S Houthakker, *The Analysis of Family Budgets*, Cambridge University Press, 1955
9   N Leviatan, 'Errors in Variables and Engel Curve Analysis', *Econometrica*, Vol 29 No 3, July 1961
10 D A Rowe, 'Private Consumption', Chapter VI of W Beckerman and Associates *The British Economy in 1975*, Cambridge University Press, 1965
11 R Stone and D H Rowe, 'Dynamic Demand Functions: some econometric results', *Economy Journal*, June 1958
12 Q Paris, *An Appraisal of Income Elasticities for total food consumption in developing countries*, OECD, 1970

Appendix E Calculation of floorspace required

An estimate of the floorspace required in 1980 can be made if the following are known:

1 Present floorspace (an estimate of this is available for England and Wales only[1])

2 Spending per head in shops in 1980 (for this purpose we use the estimates given in Chapter 4 and Appendix D).

3 Population in 1980. This is given in Table E1.

Table E1 Population estimates by region ('000)

Region	Population (1968)	Estimated population (1980)	% increase
North	3,341	3,487	4.3
Yorks/Humberside	4,804	5,047	5.0
North West	6,755	7,087	5.0
East Midlands	3,322	3,765	13.2
West Midlands	5,084	5,556	9.3
East Anglia	1,637	2,082	27.2
South East	17,230	18,435	6.9
South West	3,700	4,099	10.8
Wales	2,720	2,837	4.1
Total England and Wales	48,593	52,395	7.8
Scotland	5,188	5,337	2.9
Total Great Britain	53,781	57,732	7.1
Northern Ireland	1,502	1,718	14.3
Total United Kingdom	55,203	59,450	7.6

Sources: England and Wales: *Registrar General's Quarterly Return,* April 1969
Scotland: *Digest of Scottish Statistics,* September, 1969
Northern Ireland: *Digest of Statistics,* September 1969

1980 figures have been interpolated

4 The rate of change of shop floor utilisation sales per square foot. As explained in Chapter 4, we would estimate that the rate of increase in utilisation of existing floorspace measured in real terms, is about 1.3 per cent per annum. This means that in 1980, 1968's turnover (at current prices) could be achieved with only 85 per cent of the 1968 floorspace, provided that the present rate of change continues (see Table E2).

(It should be noted that it would have been desirable to use 'top', 'middle' and 'low' figures not only for consumers' expenditure

Table E2 Shopping floorspace in 1980

	1 Sq ft 1968	2	3 Estimated requirements (m sq ft)	4	5 Anticipated provision (m sq ft)	6	7 % difference anticipated, less required	8
		Low	Middle	High		Low	Middle	High
North	41.3	41.7	43.7	46.3	47.4	+ 13.8	+ 8.8	+ 2.2
Yorkshire/Humberside	57.4	58.0	61.4	64.9	70.0	+ 20.7	+ 14.0	+ 8.9
North West	83.1	83.9	88.9	93.9	92.2	+ 10.0	+ 3.7	— 1.9
East Midlands	34.8	38.2	40.4	42.5	43.2	+ 13.0	+ 6.9	+ 1.3
West Midlands	51.1	53.6	57.2	60.3	66.4	+ 23.9	+ 16.0	+ 10.0
East Anglia	17.9	22.1	23.3	24.5	21.6	— 2.3	— 7.3	— 11.9
South East	206.6	212.8	225.2	237.6	247.9	+ 16.4	+ 10.1	+ 4.2
South West	44.1	47.2	49.8	52.5	55.1	+ 16.8	+ 10.3	+ 5.0
Wales	28.1	28.4	29.8	31.5	32.3	+ 13.8	+ 8.3	+ 2.6
Total England and Wales	564.4	587.0	620.8	654.7	671.6	+ 14.3	+ 8.1	+ 2.7

but also for population and the rate of change of shop floor utilisation: this was not done because it involved methods of computation too sophisticated for what is at best an approximate calculation.)

Given these figures, estimates of floorspace required in 1980 may be made. These are given in columns 2, 3 and 4 of Table E2. Since 'low', 'middle' and 'high' estimates are available for spending in shops similarly characterised estimates may be made of the floorspace required in 1980.

We have not the material at our disposal to make an authoritative estimate of the amount of floorspace that will be available in 1980. What we have done for the purpose of this calculation is to assume continuance of the rate of nett increase in floorspace which obtained in the years 1964 to 1967[2] (this is a major assumption and may well be open to question: however, it is the only assumption which available information allows us to make on a quantitative basis). This estimate is given in column 5 of Table E2.

The estimates of floorspace required may then be compared with that anticipated. Columns 6 to 8 show the difference. Where the difference is positive (ie anticipated floorspace is greater than that required) there is an indication of 'excess' floorspace: however it should be stressed that this does not mean that shops, new or old will be standing vacant; it suggests that either there will be a cut-back in new construction or that there will be an acceleration of the current rate of obsolescence, ie shops in marginal areas will be converted to other uses at a higher rate than has been the case hitherto. Similarly a negative difference in columns 6 to 8 suggests acceleration of the rate of new construction or deceleration of the rate of obsolescence, ie marginal shops will be kept in use longer than hitherto. This is an important point, and is discussed in more detail in Chapter 4.

Two other points need emphasis.

First, the calculation is a crude one reflecting the unsatisfactory nature of present floorspace figures, and major assumptions have had to be made. The figures in Table E2 are probably not accurate. What is important is the *general* tendency which they illustrate. Second, the calculation does not assume that consumers' expenditure per head is uniform over the whole country, which is patently a false proposition, but it does assume that earning will increase at roughly the same pace in each region and that there will therefore be no change in the relative spending power in each region. (The evidence given by Thirlwall[3] shows that in the period from 1962 to 1968 this was roughly true.)

Conclusion   The figures in Table E2 suggest either a reduction in new construction or a marked increase in the rate of obsolescence in shops in England and Wales, with the exception of East Anglia, where the rate of increase of population forecast by the Registrar General was much the greatest in the whole country: this is an area with a high proportion of new and expanded towns. No conclusions can be drawn about Scotland or Northern Ireland, since no floorspace figures are available.

References

1 Ministry of Housing and Local Government, *Statistics for Town and Country Planning, Series* II *Floorspace,* No 2, HMSO, 1969

2 Ministry of Housing and Local Government, *Statistics for Town and Country Planning, Series* II *Floorspace,* No 1, HMSO, 1969

3 A P Thirlwall, 'Regional Phillips Curves', *Bulletin of the Oxford University Institute of Economics and Statistics,* Vol 32 No 1, February 1970

Appendix F An account of five studies undertaken to identify factors leading to success or failure in shopping centres

Five studies were undertaken, either directly by the Office, or under its auspices, with the object of identifying the reasons for success or failure in shopping centres.

The projects were as follows:

1   An examination of critical factors for success in new shopping locations, undertaken by consultants, Industrial Market Research Ltd. The objectives of the enquiry were to determine the criteria by which success and efficiency is assessed both in the retail unit and in the shopping centre itself, by different types of retailers; to isolate the pattern of opinions and attitudes towards factors considered critical to the success of shopping centres, and to test the validity of these opinions and attitudes as far as possible against objective data relating to the centres.

Four towns were surveyed: Jarrow, Derby, Norwich and Stevenage. New developments were studied in all except Norwich, where a number of older locations was also studied.

Retailers were interviewed at their shops, and key groups such as national multiples, department stores and supermarkets were also interviewed at their head offices using non-directive interview techniques.

2   An examination of retailers' views at centres in Preston, Chester, Walton-on-Thames and Redhill, undertaken directly by the Office. Broadly speaking, the object was the same as that of the consultants' survey, although the emphasis was on attitudes rather than actual performance, and was aimed at providing additional evidence for the first study in less depth but on a wider scale.

The survey was entirely structured, using a postal questionnaire.

3   An examination of new suburban shopping centres at Leeds (Crossgates), Cowley and Halesowen was conducted by staff at Leeds University under the direction of Mr J A Likierman. The emphasis here was on finding why retailers have moved to these locations and on what criteria they based their judgement.

This study involved interviews by university students, using non-directive techniques as far as possible.

4   Another project was directed at the consumer and was conducted by the Research Institute for Consumer Affairs. The terms of reference were very broadly to examine features that contribute to the pleasure and convenience of shopping, and influences affecting shopping habits. Group discussions on a number of questions were organised in Norwich and Stevenage. These provided tentative answers and suggested possible items of enquiry to be followed up by a house-to-house survey of housewives selected at random in specified districts of each town.

5   A series of pavement surveys was conducted by NEDO staff in

nine centres: Preston, Doncaster (Arndale), Doncaster (Waterdale), Derby (Duckworth Square), Chester, Walton-on-Thames, Redhill, Leeds (Crossgates) and Cowley. The object here was to provide some classification of the centres by size of catchment area, social class etc, and to provide additional evidence on a wider scale (but at a much more superficial level) for some of the RICA findings at Norwich and Stevenage.

The full results of these surveys are available on request from NEDO.

Printed in England for Her Majesty's Stationery Office
by Williams Lea/WLP Group/London